The Human Genome Project

What Does Decoding DNA Mean for Us?

Kevin Alexander Boon

Enslow Publishers, Inc.

40 Industrial Road	PO Box 38
Box 398	Aldershot
Berkeley Heights, NJ 07922	Hants GU12 6BP
USA	UK

http://www.enslow.com

Copyright © 2002 by Kevin Alexander Boon

Library of Congress Cataloging-in-Publication Data

Boon, Kevin Alexander
    The human genome project : what does decoding DNA mean for us? / Kevin Alexander Boon.
        p. cm. — (Issues in focus)
    Includes bibliographical references and index.
    Summary: Discusses genes, genetics, and the legal and ethical issues involved in mapping DNA in the human body.
    ISBN 0-7660-1685-4 (hardcover)
    1. Human Genome Project—Juvenile literature.
[1. Human Genome Project. 2. DNA. 3. Genetics.] I. Title. II. Issues in focus (Hillside, N.J.)
    QH445.2 .B66 2002
    599.93'5—dc21
                            2001003388

Printed in the United States of America

10 9 8 7 6 5 4 3 2

To Our Readers: We have done our best to make sure all Internet addresses in this book were active and appropriate when we went to press. However, the author and the publisher have no control over and assume no liability for the material available on those Internet sites or on other Web sites they may link to. Any comments or suggestions can be sent by e-mail to comments@enslow.com or to the address on the back cover.

Illustration Credits: American Cancer Society, p. 97; Corel Corp., pp. 12, 30, 38, 56, 59, 62, 67, 75, 82, 87, 101; Library of Congress, pp. 8, 43, 90; National Archives, pp. 48, 105; R. Klare, p. 17.

Cover Illustration: U.S. Department of Energy Human Genome Program.

Contents

1

To Know Ourselves

Every living thing comes with a set of instructions that determine all of its characteristics: what it looks like, how healthy it is, how intelligent it can be, and thousands of other traits. These instructions are now known as genetic information. Until the end of the twentieth century, no one knew for sure where these instructions were or what form they took. But now we do.

The Human Genome Project is a large-scale effort to record the entire set of instructions that control the development and design of a human being. Once the project is completed, scientists will have a place to search for the specific instructions that control everything from blindness to hair loss. In other words, it is only a matter of time before everything about you can be stored on a computer disk.

The possible benefits of this increased understanding of our genetic information are extensive. Genetic research will help us cure diseases and eliminate the physical suffering of hundreds of thousands of people. But there are also many dangers. Who gets access to this information? Just doctors? What about employers? The government? Insurance companies? Who owns this information and how will it be used?

It is likely that understanding the genetic information of people will lead to cures for many diseases. But the question remains, Who gets to receive these cures and who does not? Will how much money a person has determine whether or not he or she gets to live? Who will be able to make these types of decisions? If one day genetics makes it possible to double the human life span, whose life span will get doubled?

The most important issues at stake involve the rights of the individual. How will advances in genetic medicine and science affect you and me?

Early Views of Heredity

For thousands of years, people have struggled to understand the forces that make us the way we are. In ancient Greece, many believed that if the gods liked a person, he or she was blessed with strength, beauty, and health. The Greek philosopher Plato (circa 428–347 B.C.) claimed that the gods "added gold"[1] when they fashioned kings, emperors, and other rulers. According to Plato, the gods used lesser metals, such as iron or bronze, when they made farmers or shepherds.

It was assumed that the gods bestowed on people those characteristics they needed to do their jobs. Rulers were born with intelligence and sound judgment, soldiers were born with endurance and physical strength, and hunters were born with good eyesight because those were the characteristics that allowed those people to function in their occupations.

Not surprisingly, Greeks assumed that the more attractive, more intelligent, and more physically able people were, the more favored they were by the gods. The more feeble and sickly they were, the more the gods disapproved of them. And the wrath or blessings of the gods fell upon entire generations of families, because even the early civilizations noticed that children tended to resemble their parents. This was part of the rationale behind a phrase such as the playwright Euripides' "the gods visit the sins of the father upon the children."[2]

One of the earliest people to point this out was Aristotle (384–322 B.C.), one of Plato's students. Aristotle said that just as children might inherit a house from their parents, they might also inherit blue eyes or black hair. But even though people knew that

ARISTOTELES.

*Apud Fuluium Vrſinum
in marmore .*

The Greek philosopher Aristotle theorized about hereditary
traits nearly 2,400 years ago.

traits were passed from parents to children, they were stumped as to exactly how this occurred.

One early theory claimed that people began as miniature versions of themselves (each one called a homunculus). Some believed this tiny person, complete with arms, legs, and internal organs, was carried by women and fertilized by men. Others held that it was carried by men and passed to women. Once a homunculus was fertilized, it merely grew larger inside the womb until it was born.

People who believed this theory were called preformationists. Preformationists date back to the early Greek philosophers, around 300–400 b.c. The theory continued into the nineteenth century, more than 2,200 years.

Another theory, which surfaced around the same time as the theory of the preformationists, was the theory of the epigenesists. Early epigenesists argued that people did not begin as miniature copies, but developed from basic materials. The Greek philosopher Aristotle was an epigenesist. He believed that some inner force (which he called "soul") shaped people from basic materials. He held that all life began as a simple undifferentiated mass that eventually became more complex and divided into separate organs. This turned out to be the more accurate of the two theories.

One of the reasons it took so long for human beings to discover the materials that control their design is because those materials are too small to be seen with the naked eye. With the invention of the microscope in the 1590s by Zacharias and Hans Janssen, scientists were able to move beyond Aristotle's earlier theories. But there were still technical problems. The early microscopes of the sixteenth and seventeenth centuries did not magnify very well and often showed only vague, fuzzy images. As a result, many of the conclusions that Renaissance scientists reached were flawed.

It was not until the nineteenth century that microscopes became accurate enough to offer a clear look into the materials that make up human beings and other animals. And it was in the nineteenth century that the human race took its first steps toward unraveling the mystery of human life when an Augustinian monk named Gregor Mendel performed a number of experiments with the garden pea plant and unknowingly completed the first experiments in genetics. Mendel's brilliant work went virtually unnoticed until the twentieth century. Now his work marks the first step toward understanding what makes us who we are.

Evolution

Until the nineteenth century, it was generally believed that God created all living creatures and that we found these creatures as God created them. Most people believed that the physical characteristics of a particular species remained the same from generation to generation. That is, elephants always looked as they do today. So did roses. And so did human beings.

Between 1801 and 1815, a naturalist named Jean-Baptiste Lamarck (1744–1829) published his theory that species did not remain the same over time, but descended from other species. Charles Darwin (1809–1882), in his introduction to *On the Origin of Species* (1859), credits Lamarck as the "first man whose conclusions on the subject excited much attention."[3] Darwin claims that Lamarck did "eminent service of arousing attention to the probability of all change in the organic, as well as in the inorganic world, being the result of law, and not of miraculous interposition."[4] What Lamarck had done is suggest that the characteristics of living organisms were not constant. Animals (including human beings) changed over time.

Darwin, like Lamarck, was a naturalist. He examined and catalogued animals from all over the world. From his observations, Darwin concluded that species did evolve over time, as Lamarck had suggested, but that those changes were not the result of the "will" of the species. According to Darwin, species underwent change as a result of a principle known as natural selection, which "explains the grouping of all organic beings."[5]

The theory of natural selection predicts that characteristics that allow an organism to survive are passed on to that organism's offspring. Over time, species can transform into new species based on which characteristics were passed on. As Darwin puts it:

As many more individuals of each species are born than can possibly survive; and as, consequently, there is a frequently recurring struggle for existence, it follows that any being, if it vary however slightly in any manner profitable to itself, under the complex and sometimes varying conditions of life, will have a better chance of surviving, and thus be naturally selected.[6]

One example that some scientists saw as natural selection at work involves "peppered" moths in England. These moths come in both light and dark varieties. Researchers argued that prior to the

After studying such animals as this Galapagos tortoise, Charles Darwin developed the theory that major changes in the structure of animals are related to the environment of those animals and their ancestors.

industrialization of England in the nineteenth century, the light-colored variety vastly outnumbered the dark-colored variety. With industrialization came factories that poured soot and pollutants into the air. As a result, the light-colored lichen that had covered trees was killed off and the pollution in the air turned the bark of the trees dark. Researchers found that near industrial cities, dark-colored moths soon greatly outnumbered light-colored moths, and "by 1900, 98% of the moths in the vicinity of English cities . . . were mostly black."[7]

The reason claimed for this change was that when the trees darkened, dark-colored moths were harder for predators to see, while light-colored moths stood out. Therefore, more dark-colored moths survived to reproduce.

Although this peppered moth story generated a great deal of excitement in scientific circles, it has since been dismissed as inaccurate and possibly fraudulent science.[8] Scientists are still searching for a conclusive example of natural selection.

The results of the Human Genome Project will be of tremendous importance to understanding the evolution of human beings. Because human evolution took place over thousands of years, we cannot see the changes take place as we can with bacteria (which, because of its short life span, can be "evolved" in a day or two). Nevertheless, our DNA and the DNA of our ancestors carry the history of our evolution. It will soon be possible to accurately compare the DNA found in prehistoric bones to the DNA of people living today. The results will not only tell us if we are genetically related to those bones, but they will also be able to tell us who living today is most closely related to the person from whom those bones came.

The same is true for animals. If human beings and chimpanzees descended from common ancestors, DNA may be able to trace that connection and perhaps locate where the two species took separate paths.

2

Understanding Genes and Genetics

Gregor Mendel (1823–1884) was a simple, unassuming man who wore round, gold-rimmed spectacles. Although he studied science and mathematics at the University of Vienna, he was not formally a scientist. He was a religious man, a monk of the Augustinian order established by the pope in 1244 A.D. But Mendel was interested in heredity, or how characteristics are passed from parents to their offspring. In the mid-nineteenth century, he began a series of experiments with pea plants. He could often be found in his black tunic, tending rows of pea plants

15

beneath the clock tower outside the library of the Augustinian monastery in Brünn, Moravia (now Brno in the Czech Republic), where he lived most of his life.

Mendel was searching for evidence for Jean-Baptiste Lamarck's theory of evolution. Lamarck believed that traits were inherited based on need. For example, he argued that giraffes developed long necks because they *needed* to reach leaves higher in trees. Mendel designed his experiments with pea plants to track traits through several generations.

Mendel's experiments are good examples of the scientific method. The scientific method is a process for testing a hypothesis. A hypothesis is a statement made as if the statement were true for the purpose of testing that statement. For example, "Two objects of unequal weight will fall at the same rate" is a hypothesis. If you have never seen your dog eat carrots, so is "My dog does not like carrots."

Once a hypothesis is formed, experiments can be designed to test the hypothesis. If you wanted to test the hypothesis that your dog does not like carrots, you might try to feed him carrots at every meal for a week and record whether or not he eats them. If he never eats them, you could conclude that he does not like them. If he eats them only in the afternoon, you might amend your hypothesis: "My dog eats carrots only in the afternoon."

If you wanted to test the hypothesis that two objects of unequal weight fall at the same rate, you might take a bowling ball and a tennis ball, drop them both at the same time, and watch to see if they hit the ground together.

What Gregor Mendel did is take pea plants with contrasting characteristics. For example, in one set of experiments he took plants that always produced round peas and bred them with plants that always produced dented peas. This created a hybrid pea

Gregor Mendel's experiments with pea plants mark the beginning of classical genetics.

plant—a pea plant whose parents have different characteristics.

Mendel called the first generation of offspring the F_1 generation. He then bred pea plants from the F_1 generation together to produce an F_2 generation.

Mendel discovered two important facts about heredity from his experiments. His first discovery was that the first generation always exhibited one of the two traits. In his experiments with round and dented peas, the F_1 generation all had round peas. Because the trait for round peas seemed to dominate the trait for dented peas, he labeled it the "dominant trait."

Mendel's second discovery was that in the F_2 generation, the dominant trait appeared in roughly 75 percent of the offspring. The other 25 percent exhibited the trait that had been dominated. He labeled this trait the "recessive trait." Because the trait for round peas was dominant in Mendel's pea plants, the first generation of offspring all had round peas, but they carried the traits for round and dented. The second generation of offspring had round and dented peas, with round pea plants outnumbering dented pea plants three to one.

He found the same pattern with stem length. In his 1865 paper *Experiments in Plant Hybridization,* he notes that "in repeated experiments, stems of 1 ft. and 6 ft. in length yielded without exception hybrids which varied in length between 6 ft. and 7½ ft."[1]

Mendel worked for eight years on his pea plants before he formally revealed the results of his experiments to the local scientific community in 1865. By

R = Dominant trait for round peas
d = Recessive trait for dented peas

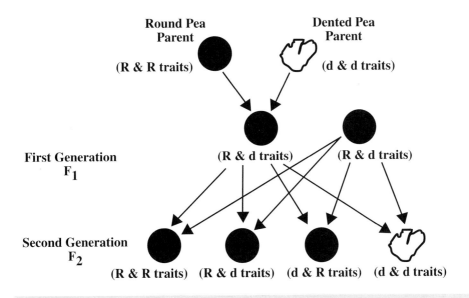

then he had tracked seven traits in his pea plants: height, pea shape, pod color, flower position, pea texture (wrinkled or smooth), stem length, and unripe pod color. What he discovered by studying these seven traits was the patterns by which characteristics were passed from parent plants to their offspring.

Mendel's experiments showed a relationship between plants and their previous generations. Messages were being passed from parents to offspring in an organized and predictable way.

However, the mechanisms that sent these messages from one generation to the next were still unknown. These messages are what we now call genes.

Each of the seven traits that Mendel manipulated is controlled by a single gene. This made it possible for his simple experiments to yield results. However, most traits involve a number of genes. The color of a mouse's coat, for example, is determined by sixty-three genes.[2]

The term "genetics" did not appear until 1906, and the term "gene" did not appear until 1909, nearly half a century after Mendel completed his important paper on heredity. Nevertheless, his work with pea plants marks the beginning of the field of genetics.

Flies' Eyes

In the nineteenth century, scientists discovered that living creatures were made up of cells. This was the start of a field of science known as cell biology. Cell biologists discovered that each cell contained a nucleus and that the nucleus contained objects, which they called chromosomes. Chromosomes are small thread-like bodies, which contain our DNA. Two of these chromosomes, X and Y, were discovered to determine the sex of an offspring.

Between 1900 and 1910, scientists firmly established the connection between chromosomes and genes, launching the most active period of classical genetics. Robert P. Wagner, Professor Emeritus of Zoology at the University of Texas and former president of the Genetics Society of America, tells us that classical genetics "refers to those aspects of genetics that can be studied without reference to the molecular details of genes."[3] This means that classical geneticists would experiment by watching the change and evolution in an organism from generation to generation.

In 1910, a classical geneticist named Thomas Hunt Morgan began to experiment with fruit flies *(Drosophila)*. Morgan was interested in proving Charles Darwin's theory that major changes in the structure of animals "are in some way due to the nature of the conditions of life, to which the parents and their more remote ancestors have been exposed during several generations."[4]

Like many scientists working with heredity in the first decade of the twentieth century, Morgan experimented with fruit flies because they were easy to feed, took up very little space (thousands could be kept in small bottles and jars), and could create a new generation in only ten days. In a single year, Morgan could watch the development of thirty-six generations. It takes humans around one thousand years to move through thirty-six generations.

When he began his experiments, Morgan's fruit flies all had red eyes, but after two years of frustrating research, he finally managed to breed a mutation: a fly with white eyes. He accomplished this by exposing his flies to various environmental factors such as radiation and chemicals (X rays, acids, radium, and alkalis). He then bred the new fly with white eyes to a fly with red eyes, and thereby introduced the new trait into the species. Before long he had thousands of white-eyed flies. Morgan's white-eyed flies showed that new traits could appear in a species as a result of changes in the environment, just as Darwin had predicted fifty-one years earlier.

Many of Morgan's results matched Mendel's results with pea plants, but some of his results were different. For example, Morgan discovered that not all traits were independent of each other. He discovered that a fly with white eyes was more likely to be male than female, which showed that the trait for maleness and the trait for white eyes were linked. Because white eyes occurred more frequently in male flies, Morgan knew that the gene that determined eye color in the fruit flies had to be located on the chromosome that determined maleness. This resulted in Morgan's most important contribution to genetics: raising the possibility that genes were located in chromosomes in the nucleus of a cell.

In 1944, a scientist named Oswald Avery published his research on bacteria. Avery's results showed that genes, the genetic messengers, were indeed located on chromosomes. Avery's research further showed that genes were not made of protein, as nearly everyone in the scientific community believed at the time. Genes were made of deoxyribonucleic acid, or DNA.

Understanding DNA

People have known for thousands of years that traits are passed from parents to their children, but it was not until the twentieth century that we began to understand exactly how this happens.

Scientists discovered that the instructions, or genetic code, for human beings are located inside the body's cells. The human body is made up of 75 trillion individual cells. Each cell has a nucleus, and our genetic code is found in the nucleus of each cell (except red blood cells). These instructions come in the form of chemicals, which form the structure we know as DNA. The term "genome" refers to the entire set of instructions.

The arrangement of chemicals in the human genome is surprisingly simple, considering that these chemicals are responsible for everything from the color of a person's eyes to how many freckles are on the back of his or her hand.

There are only four chemicals directly involved in the basic code that makes up DNA. They are adenine, thymine, cytosine, and guanine. These four chemicals are called bases. When one of these is combined with a sugar (a combination, or compound, of carbon, hydrogen, and oxygen) and a phosphate (a compound of phosphoric acid), the result is called a nucleotide.

The chemical adenine and the chemical thymine always bond with each other. The chemical cytosine and the chemical guanine always bond with each other. The smallest particle of each chemical you can have is called a molecule.

The four bases (adenine, thymine, cytosine, and guanine) are organized as pairs on strands of DNA. Each pair of molecules is called a base pair. Because adenine and thymine always bond together and cytosine and guanine always bond together, a base pair consists of either a molecule of adenine and a molecule of thymine or a molecule of cytosine and a molecule of guanine.

Each base pair (adenine and thymine or cytosine and guanine) in a strand of DNA is located between a sugar molecule and a phosphate molecule. So the four possible base pairs are:

1. cytosine (C) and guanine (G)

2. guanine (G) and cytosine (C)

3. adenine (A) and thymine (T)

4. thymine (T) and adenine (A)

Base pairs are found in a sequence, which, when untwisted, resembles a ladder. It takes an average of three thousand base pairs to make up a gene. The entire human genome consists of about 3 billion base pairs.

Each strand of DNA is made up of thousands and thousands of base pairs, and each strand is twisted together with another strand to form the double-stranded molecule that makes up DNA.

In 1953, James Watson and Francis Crick discovered that DNA was shaped like a ladder twisted into a double helix, similar in appearance to a spiral staircase. Watson said, recalling the day of the discovery, "We had found the secret of life."[5] Their discovery confirmed DNA's role as the carrier of hereditary information. In 1962, Watson and Crick were awarded a Nobel Prize (along with Maurice Hugh Frederick Wilkins) for their discovery. In 1988, Watson became the head of the U.S. Human Genome Project (he later resigned).

A section, or sequence, of DNA makes up a gene. Many genes are linked to form chromosomes. These chromosomes are arranged in pairs.

Every living organism has a fixed number of chromosomes. Human beings have twenty-three pairs of chromosomes. One pair of chromosomes carries genetic information about our gender; the other twenty-two carry the genetic information controlling everything else. When one gene occupies the same place on a specific chromosome as another gene that produces a different characteristic, it is called an allele. If, for example, the gene for green eyes is located at the same place on a chromosome as the gene for blue eyes, this would be considered an allele.

When human cells reproduce, each new cell receives an entire copy of all the chromosomes. This means that each cell contains the entire DNA or all the information about a person.

When people reproduce, a single set of their chromosomes unravels. Half of the father's DNA and half of the mother's DNA combine to form the DNA of the child. Through this means, children inherit half of their characteristics from their father and half from their mother.

Our DNA is like a giant blueprint controlling how we grow and develop as individuals and as a species. The more we understand about our own genetic code, the more control we have over human growth and development. Knowing where the gene for a disease such as cancer or Alzheimer's is located may eventually allow us to replace the Alzheimer's gene with a healthier gene, effectively curing the disease. We may one day be able to do this for every genetic disease. This prospect excites many people. But there are others who feel that exposing the secrets of our genetic code might lead to dangerous consequences, such as the cloning of human beings for spare parts.

3

The Human Genome Project

The Human Genome Project (HGP) began in 1990 with a projected cost of $3 billion, or "$200 million per year for approximately 15 years."[1] Its primary goal is to map the entire genetic code for a human being. This genetic map will provide scientists with the information they need to identify the estimated thirty to forty thousand genes that control human characteristics.

When the project is complete, the world will finally have a rough copy of the genetic instruction manual for human beings. The U.S. Department of Energy explains that the primary aim of the project is "to obtain a word-by-word copy of the entire genetic script for an 'average' human being."[2]

Advances in technology have sped up the process so much that the Human Genome Project, which was not expected to complete its initial sequencing of the human genome until 2005, has leaped ahead of schedule. The project reached a major milestone in April 1998 when it crossed the halfway point. On June 26, 2000, the National Institutes of Health (NIH) and Celera Genomics Group (a private corporation) jointly announced that the project had completed the first rough draft of the genome a year earlier than initially planned. President Bill Clinton referred to it as a "landmark achievement, which promises to lead to a new era of molecular medicine, an era that will bring new ways to prevent, diagnose, treat and cure disease."[3] Estimates now indicate that the project should be done by 2003.

Who Is Working on the HGP?

The Human Genome Project was initiated by the United States, but it is an international enterprise involving more than eighteen countries. Some of the countries collaborating with the United States on the project are Brazil, Australia, China, France, Denmark, Sweden, Netherlands, Mexico, Japan, Korea, Canada, Germany, Russia, Israel, Italy, and the United Kingdom. Scientists from around the world are cooperating to complete the code. Some work for governmental agencies, universities, and private corporations. Others work for organizations formed solely for the purpose of sequencing the human genome. The most influential private company working on the genome is Celera, which is headed by J. Craig Venter.

The Goals of the Project

The project involves more than the identification and sequencing of the estimated 30,000–40,000 genes and the 3 billion chemical bases that make up the human genome. Scientists working on the project must determine the best methods for storing all this information in databases. They are also striving to develop machines and software to sequence genetic material more quickly and analyze the massive amount of information the project will generate.

In addition to completing a map of the human genome by 2003, one of the goals of the Human Genome Project is to "make the sequence totally and freely available."[4] To do this, people working with the project are creating "public resources of DNA samples and cell lines." Behind this goal is the idea that everyone should be able to get information on the human genome. No single group of people—not scientists, corporations, or countries—should be able to control the information the project learns about our genetic makeup.

The Human Genome Project also actively supports the training of scholars and new scientists skilled in genetic research in issues related to genetics, such as ethics, the social sciences, and law. This

Slight differences in the structure of DNA result in superficial differences in the way people look.

is all in preparation for the explosion in genetic biology that many predict will occur in the twenty-first century.

One unique goal of the project is its attempt to address the legal, social, and ethical issues that may arise out of the project's efforts. The Human Genome Project is the first large-scale scientific project to consider how its discoveries may affect people around the world. Scientists and scholars working on the project are not only concerned with acquiring new knowledge about the genes that control human development, they are equally concerned with the effect this knowledge will have on people. Once we understand and are able to manipulate the code that controls human life, how should this information be used? What possible impact will it have on societies worldwide?

Predicting the Future

We cannot know for certain the wide-sweeping impact the Human Genome Project will have, but those familiar with the science of genetics can make educated predictions. Francis Collins, the head of the National Institutes of Health's role in the project, and Walter Gilbert, a 1980 Nobel Prize laureate for his work in genetic chemistry, jointly made the following predictions:

- By the year 2000

  Scientists will have deciphered the genetic codes for twenty to fifty hereditary diseases which have caused untold suffering since the dawn of humanity, including cystic fibrosis, muscular dystrophy, sickle-cell anemia, Tay-Sachs disease, hemophilia, and Huntington's chorea.

- Prior to 2006

The 100,000 or so genes [the number of genes previously believed to make up the genome] that make up the human genome will have been deciphered by the Human Genome Project, which will open up the secrets locked for millions of years in our genes.

- By the year 2010

The genetic profiles of hereditary diseases will balloon to approximately 2,000 to 5,000, giving us an almost complete understanding of the genetic basis of these ancient diseases.[5]

Collins claims that by the year 2010 "you will be able to have your own report card printed out of your individual risks for future disease based on the genes you have inherited." By 2020 or 2030, Collins says, "You'll be able to go to a drugstore and get your own DNA sequence on a CD, which you can then analyze at home on your Macintosh."[6]

Many of Collins and Gilbert's predictions for the year 2000 have already come true. Whether or not the others will remains to be seen. But one thing is certain: Our lives and our cultures will be substantially different by the middle of the twenty-first century as a result of the Human Genome Project.

Health, Eugenics, and Genetic Counseling

4

The completion of the Human Genome Project could revolutionize the field of health care. Thomas H. Murray, the director of the Center for Biomedical Ethics at Case Western Reserve University and a founding member of the Ethical, Legal, and Social Issues Working Group for the Human Genome Project, claims that the project will "reshape health care in the United States." He argues that the project will "substantially alter the Who, the What, and the To Whom, and may also affect the At Whose Expense."[1] What Murray means by this is that the Human

Genome Project will prompt changes in *who* provides health care in the twenty-first century, *what* type of health care they provide, *to whom* this health care is provided, and *who* ultimately pays for it.

Murray projects that all four of these areas of health care will change drastically. Exactly how they will change is unsure, but once the map of the human genome offers new ways of thinking about illness and health, the fact that they will change is certain.

One place we can expect change is in the relationship between physicians and their patients. For years this relationship has involved the diagnosis and treatment of disease. People got sick, went to a doctor, and the doctor treated their illnesses. But what about treating disease before a patient becomes ill? What about eliminating the possibility that a patient will contract a disease?

Since the 1970s, many physicians have been aware of preventive medicine, but the tools at their disposal have been limited to general guidelines regarding diet, exercise, and the avoidance of potentially dangerous environments. Doctors had very little ability to predict who might get certain diseases, although the medical field has long been aware of genetic links to certain ailments, such as sickle-cell anemia and hemophilia.

Sickle-cell anemia is a disease that interferes with the flow of red blood cells; it occurs primarily in people of African descent. Hemophilia, a disease in which blood does not clot, is passed from mothers almost exclusively to their male offspring. A person of African descent with a family history of sickle-cell anemia would be considered part of a high-risk group and might contract the disease at some point in his or her life. But it is also possible that a man or woman from such a background may not get the disease. The same is true for families with a history of hemophilia. Prior to genetics, physicians could not know with any confidence what to expect until after their patients got ill. The Human Genome Project may very well change all of that.

Diagnosing and Treating Disease

Genetics may make it possible to diagnose and treat diseases long before people get sick. It may even become possible to diagnose and treat diseases before a person is born. Because your genetic code holds the blueprint for your entire body, unraveling its secrets will allow physicians to determine which diseases you may contract and repair those genes before they have the opportunity to make you ill.

How quickly the genes controlling a disease are identified and some form of treatment is devised depends greatly on how many genes are involved. The relationship between a genetic disease and the genetic makeup of a person varies. All of the following are possible:

- A disease may be determined by only one gene (homozygous diseases).

- A disease may be determined by a combination of genes.

• The genes related to a disease may interact with environmental factors.

If a disease is controlled by one gene (or one allele), then once that gene is located, a treatment may be devised. If a disease is controlled by a combination of genes, then it becomes increasingly difficult to pin down the genetics of that disease. And if the genes interact with environmental factors, then someone, under the right environmental circumstances, may carry the genes for a disease without actually getting it.

Geneticists have already identified the genes for a number of diseases, including sickle-cell anemia and some forms of hemophilia. Gene therapy may very soon put an end to the suffering caused by these diseases. It is also being considered for a "wide array of disorders including kidney stones and arthritis."[2]

Experimental gene therapies are already being tried. Scientists at the National Institutes of Health (NIH) introduced the gene for a particular viral enzyme (herpes simplex thymidine kinase) directly into a brain tumor in an attempt to kill the tumor with antiviral drugs without harming the surrounding brain tissue.[3] The experiment had promising results.

Several researchers are working on possible gene therapies for AIDS (acquired immunodeficiency syndrome). One group genetically alters white blood cells in a laboratory and then replaces them in a patient's bloodstream. White blood cells are the body's defense against germs and infections. When a germ enters the bloodstream, the white blood cells have several ways of combating it. If the researchers are successful, the altered cells will possess an increased ability to defend against the AIDS virus. A viral enzyme is also introduced (the same one used by the NIH in its brain tumor experiments) into the cells. If the introduction of the altered white blood cells fails to work, this enzyme, appropriately called a "suicide vector," will allow researchers to selectively destroy the altered cells with antiviral drugs.[4]

Gene therapies are being developed for a broad range of diseases, including cancer, coronary heart disease (which often leads to heart attacks), and infectious diseases. If these new therapies are successful, as many predict they will be, the Human Genome Project will have fulfilled what William J. Polvino and W. French Anderson consider the project's ethical foundation: It will have helped to relieve human suffering.[5]

The World Health Organization (WHO) expects the project results to provide tremendous possibilities for the prevention, diagnosis, and treatment of inherited diseases and a wide spectrum of other diseases. They expect medical care to have an increased power to prevent disease before the disease manifests symptoms. If we can predict a disease before it springs to life, then we may very well be able to cure it before it threatens a person's physical well-being. WHO also expects the technology developed during the Human Genome Project to aid in the development and production of drugs and vaccines.[6]

Because of the widespread significance of the

It is likely that parents will soon be able to alter the DNA of their children before they are born.

Human Genome Project, WHO calls for the development of health policies that take into consideration ethical, medical, and social concerns and the rights of the individual.[7]

Controlling Heredity

In the latter half of the nineteenth century, before the word "gene" was a part of our vocabulary and long before anyone knew anything about chromosomes and DNA, Charles Darwin's cousin, Francis Galton, argued that we could improve the quality of people by controlling who was allowed to have children and with whom they were allowed to reproduce (a practice called selective breeding). Galton based his ideas on statistical averages. He experimented with sweet peas and a device he called a quincunx. A quincunx was a simple box with a glass front. Lead shot of equal weight could be dropped into the box where it would fall through a series of pins. Each ball of lead had an equal probability of landing on the left or the right of the box.

Galton discovered that how the balls fell into his quincunx would vary slightly from experiment to experiment, but that overall they would tend to clump together. If you dropped one hundred balls into the machine, one time you might get a distribution of forty-eight on the left and fifty-two on the right. The next time you might get fifty-six on the left and forty-four on the right. But over time, you would *tend* to get, on average, fifty on the left and fifty on the right.

Adolphe Quetelet, a Belgian mathematician and astronomer, had made a similar discovery many years before. Quetelet was one of the first people to apply statistical reasoning to social phenomena. One of his experiments involved measuring the chest size of Scottish soldiers. Although chest size varied from experiment to experiment, it tended to clump around an average. His measurements of the chest size of Scottish soldiers, for example, showed that if he measured a thousand men or a hundred men he would still tend to get the same average chest size. Although chest size varied from individual soldier to individual soldier, it remained constant across groups. This led

Quetelet to theorize that all human characteristics—both physical and mental—had consistent averages. To Quetelet's mind, the idea of an "average man" was not merely an abstract concept, but a real set of measurable characteristics.

Quetelet's concept of an average man and Darwin's theory of evolution led Galton to the eventual conclusion that the whole of humanity could be improved if these measurements were used to determine which physical and mental characteristics should be passed to future generations and which should not. Galton argued that people could consciously influence the course of their own evolution.

Galton came to believe that many characteristics were a result of heredity—for instance, that it was the reason that the sons of distinguished men tended to distinguish themselves. In an 1864 article in *MacMillan's Magazine,* Galton claimed:

> A man must inherit good health, a love of mental work, a strong purpose, and considerable ambition, in order to achieve successes of the high order of which we are speaking. The deficiency of any one of these qualities would certainly be injurious, and probably be fatal to his chance of obtaining great distinction.[8]

Galton felt that breeding could improve a human being's chances of being a successful member of society. His theories were used to justify the assumed supremacy of Western European aristocracy.

Eugenics

The theories of men such as Galton led to the development of the field of eugenics, the formal study of ways to improve the human characteristics we inherit. The term was coined by Galton in 1886. It comes from the Greek and literally means "good origin" or "good generation."

The American eugenics movement began at the close of the Civil War and reached its peak in the 1920s. Industrialization was beginning, and the working class was growing at a rate that alarmed members of the wealthy upper class. By the beginning of the twentieth century, a great deal of data about different ethnic groups was collected and mistakenly presented as evidence of the superiority of white Western Europeans. Nearly all of this "scientific" data has since been discredited, but during the first half of the twentieth century, much of it was considered scientific fact. From 1910 to 1940, the Eugenics Record Office in Cold Spring Harbor, New York, archived thousands of articles, pedigrees, and charts, all of which were presumed to distinguish people who had "good" genes from those who had "bad" genes.

Charles Davenport (1866–1944), a renowned biologist at the turn of the century and director of the biological research center at Cold Springs Harbor, was one of the foremost advocates of eugenics and one of Galton's followers. Inspired by the recently rediscovered work of Gregor Mendel, Davenport set out to find a way to predict human characteristics.

But unlike Mendel's pea plants, people could not be bred in scientific experiments. So Davenport studied family histories, tracing characteristics that recurred from generation to generation. His research included physical characteristics and diseases, such as hemophilia, but it also attempted to trace inherited criminal behavior and mental retardation.

Davenport and others like him were excited by the notion that people could be improved. But genetics was a new field and the science had a long way to go before the genetic source of specific traits could be identified. Thus, much of the eugenics movement mixed together the little science that was available at the time and social attitudes.

The Dark Side of Eugenics

At the opening of the twentieth century, the eugenics movement argued that some groups of people, as a whole, inherited better characteristics than others. Most of those who were drawn to eugenics were Western European, so perhaps we should not be too surprised that those of good "racial stock" turned out to be people of Western European heritage, just like Davenport and others researching family histories.

It was not long before the thrust of the eugenics movement turned ugly, offering "scientific" support for racial and national prejudices that already existed. A great many people of various nationalities immigrated to the United States during the first part of the twentieth century, and this sudden influx of foreigners disturbed many Americans. The poorly

Many immigrants who arrived at Ellis Island seeking American citizenship were denied entry based on unfair intelligence tests that supposedly revealed they were of "inferior stock."

supported claims of organizations such as the American Eugenics Society gave people excuses for dismissing the new Americans as being of inferior stock.

In addition to promoting the breeding of people from "superior" stock, the eugenics movement also wanted to restrict the breeding of people of "inferior" stock. People whose heritage contained a history of disease, such as epilepsy or hemophilia, were discouraged from having children. But those advocating eugenics did not stop there; they also tried to discourage people with a history of alcoholism from having children, as well as people with a history of poverty. Coming from a poor family was enough of a reason to be considered bad stock. Davenport said, "Society must protect itself," and argued that just as society had the "right to deprive the murderer of his life so also may it annihilate the hideous serpent of hopelessly vicious protoplasm."[9] Davenport meant that we do not let murderers keep on murdering, so why should we let people who carry bad traits continue to pass them on to future generations?

All immigrants were fair game, and the eugenics movement labeled all people from southern Europe, Asia, and Africa as inferior. Like Davenport, Henry Goddard (1866–1957), a psychologist and former schoolteacher, was taken with the idea of genes and heredity, particularly as they related to intelligence. He used the Binet Simon intelligence test to estimate the intelligence of a wide variety of people, including prison inmates, residents at homes for wayward girls, and patients at the Training School for Feeble-Minded Boys and Girls in Vineland, New Jersey.

Between 1892 and the mid-1950s, millions of immigrants, most from European countries, entered the United States through Ellis Island in New York. Goddard saw this as an opportunity to test the intelligence of people of different nationalities. He administered intelligence tests to a small number of them. Most of the immigrants, who were unfamiliar with both American culture and the English language, did poorly on the tests. Although Goddard acknowledged that a lack of knowledge about American culture could affect how well people scored on the exams, he still wrongly concluded that some 80 percent of Italians, Russians, and Jews were mentally deficient, and he used these results and his influence to limit the entry of many Eastern Europeans into the United States.

Goddard was a racist who used pseudoscientific ideas about heredity to falsely legitimize his ideas. He claimed, "The average intellectual standard of the Negro is some two grades below our own [white Western Europeans'],” and in 1884, he said, "The Jews are specialized for parasitical existence upon other nations."[10]

Goddard wanted to make sure that feebleminded people did not have children. He thought that if he could prevent the reproduction of these "inferiors," he could eliminate feeblemindedness in one generation. Because the public would not accept mass sterilization, Goddard promoted the building of asylums where the mentally inadequate could be housed and kept from reproducing. A wide variety of people were placed in these institutions. Among them were those suffering from depression, blindness, perceived mental deficiency, alcoholism, epilepsy, and many other conditions that eugenicists saw as a threat to the human gene pool.

Goddard's ideas helped spread the racist message of eugenics. The results were horrifying. In the 1890s, one superintendent of a home for the feebleminded castrated fifty-eight children before public reaction forced him to stop. In 1898, the Michigan legislature considered a bill that would permit the castration (surgical removal of the testes or ovaries) of all inmates of the Michigan Home for the Feebleminded and Epileptic. In 1907, Indiana passed a law making sterilization compulsory for "confirmed criminals, idiots, rapists and imbeciles" in state institutions. In 1932, at the Third International Congress of Eugenics in New York, Dr. Theodore Russell Roble of the Essex County Mental Hygiene Clinic in New Jersey "called for the sterilization of at least 14 million Americans who had received low intelligence scores since World War I."[11]

Laws were passed in nearly half the states in America to authorize the sterilization of undesirable people, ultimately resulting in the sterilization of more than thirty-six thousand people.

The Nazis adopted the ideas of eugenics into their philosophy. Hitler's 1933 law, "The Nazi Act for Averting Descendants Afflicted with Hereditary

Diseases," was based closely on Henry H. Laughlin's Model Eugenical Sterilization Law, which called for the mandatory sterilization of a wide range of people, including drug users, those with impaired vision, the crippled, orphans, the poor, and the homeless. Hitler's law resulted in the forced sterilization of 375,000 people by 1939.

Nazis were attempting to create a pure Aryan "master race" by controlling who was allowed to reproduce and by slaughtering people they considered to be of inferior stock. The result was the Holocaust, during which millions of people died, many of whom were Jews and Gypsies.

The Holocaust shocked people around the world, and the eugenics movement no longer had much support. After the end of World War II, the idea of eugenics was no longer associated with the betterment of the human race; it was associated with cruel injustice and mass murder.

Banking the Future of Humanity

Although the atrocities of World War II put an end to eugenics as a nationally supported movement in America, the idea that we could improve the human race by consciously deciding which genes to pass on continued. In 1980, Robert Graham, who became wealthy by inventing shatterproof eyeglasses, decided to invest part of his fortune in the betterment of humankind. What Graham did was set up a sperm bank, which collected sperm from winners of the Nobel Prize, professors, and scientists. This

The Nazis, led by Adolf Hitler, adopted the ideas of eugenics into their philosophy and killed millions during the Holocaust in their attempt to create a pure Aryan "master race."

sperm was made available to qualified women who wanted to have children. Interested women were given questionnaires, which asked them about their health and any history of disease that might run in their families. Women with a history of hereditary disease in their family were rejected. Those who were deemed acceptable were artificially inseminated.

By the time Graham died, more than 230 children had been conceived from the sperm of geniuses. Many of these children did indeed excel in academics. Graham himself admitted that you could not make a genius, but he did say that "you can increase the odds dramatically by using the sperm from highly intelligent men."[12]

Graham's project died with him, but what happens when the Human Genome Project is complete? It is possible the genes controlling intelligence will eventually be located and mapped. Then it *will* be possible to make a genius. But genetically making geniuses, many people have pointed out, runs the risk of creating a new genetic class system, wherein the wealthy and powerful improve their genetic pool while the poor become further excluded from the halls of power and influence. Philosopher Gregory Kavka argues that "old aristocracies of birth, color, or gender may dissipate, only to be replaced by a new genetic aristocracy, or 'genetocracy.'"[13]

Genetic Counseling

After the atrocities of Adolf Hitler were exposed at the end of World War II, the public and most scientists rejected eugenics. But there was still a strong interest in understanding the connection between genes and disease.

In 1947, at the University of Minnesota, Sheldon Reed, a geneticist, came up with the term "genetic counseling" to describe a new field of health care that developed to help families understand how their family backgrounds potentially put them at risk for particular diseases.[14] Unlike eugenics, which sought to control the genetic development of people, genetic counseling was neutral. Reed explains that the role of a genetic counselor is to "explain thoroughly what the genetic situation is but the decision must be a personal one between the husband and wife, and theirs alone."[15]

Early genetic counselors worked in hereditary counseling clinics. They tried to determine a family's risk for genetic diseases and birth defects by analyzing family histories. Because so little was known about the actual genetic makeup of human beings, these counselors dealt primarily with simple, well-known diseases, most of which were controlled by a single gene. They were relatively successful at predicting common diseases such as sickle-cell anemia, but they were not very accurate when it came to predicting more complex diseases and disorders (such as breast cancer and asthma), particularly ones originating from two healthy parents.

From the end of World War II until 1967, there were only a handful of clinics with genetic counselors. But in 1967, medical science developed a genetic test that could be performed on pregnant women. The test is called amniocentesis. A physician inserts a long needle through a pregnant woman's abdomen into her uterus and withdraws a small amount of the fluid surrounding her unborn baby. This substance, amniotic fluid, contains cells from the unborn baby. Each cell contains the baby's chromosomes. In a laboratory, the chromosomes are analyzed in order to locate abnormalities that could result in birth defects.

Locating genetic abnormalities was only part of the process. After the test was complete, the results of genetic testing had to be relayed to parents. The role of genetic counselors in health care became more important. It was their job to explain to patients what the results of genetic tests were and what those results meant.

By the end of the 1960s, college degrees in genetic counseling became available. In 1975, the American Society of Human Genetics (ASHG) offered an updated definition of genetic counseling. According to the ASHG,

> genetic counseling is a communication process which deals with the human problems associated with the occurrence, or risk of occurrence, of a genetic disorder in a family. The process of genetic counseling involves an attempt by one or more appropriately trained individuals to help the affected individual or family to:
>
> 1. understand the medical facts, including the diagnosis, probable course of the disorder, and what they can do to manage the disease;
>
> 2. understand the relationship between heredity and the disorder and the risk of the disease occurring in specific relatives;
>
> 3. understand the alternatives for dealing with the risk of the disease appearing;
>
> 4. choose a course of action which seems to be appropriate in view of their risk, their family goals, and their ethical and religious standards, and act in accordance with that decision; and

> 5. make the best possible adjustment to the disorder in an affected family member and/or to the risk of that disorder reocurring.[16]

The more scientists learn about our genetic code, the more involved genetic counseling becomes. Individuals and families may seek genetic counseling today to determine their risk of developing disorders late in life. Amniocentesis, for example, can detect the probability that a fetus, if born, will develop problems, such as Alzheimer's disease, forty or fifty years into its life.[17] As we learn more about the genes that determine our development, genetic counseling will be able to tell us more and more about our health and the health of our children.

Many groups and organizations recognize the complicated ethical problems that this information raises. Before genetics began to unravel the secrets of human DNA, people were in the dark as to what might happen to them. Now they can tell a great deal about what may happen over the course of their lives, and they can make decisions based on that information. But what decisions are appropriate? If parents learn that their unborn baby has an 80 percent chance of developing Alzheimer's disease by the age of fifty, what action should they take? Some may choose to have an abortion, despite the fact that someone with an 80 percent chance of contracting Alzheimer's may never actually get the disease, whereas someone with a 20 percent chance might. Just because a disease is probable does not mean it is inevitable.

The environment also influences the way we

develop. A person may have the genes for a disease, but if he or she is not exposed to environmental conditions that trigger the disease, he or she will remain healthy.

Ethical concerns get even more complicated when we consider other characteristics that genetics can predict. It is already possible to find out the sex of an unborn child with relative certainty by analyzing the DNA found in amniotic fluid. Parents who want a boy may decide to abort a pregnancy based solely on those test results. Many people question whether or not that is right. Some claim it is the equivalent of murder.

One thing is certain: The more we know and the more we are able to determine by analyzing our genetic material, the more difficult the decisions people will have to face. And in the twenty-first century, genetic counseling will play an increasingly important role in those decisions.

5

The Project's Effect on Industry and Science

New technology and resources resulting from the Human Genome Project will have a major impact on industry worldwide. Some visionaries predict that these new technologies and DNA-based products will result in sales exceeding $45 billion by the year 2009.[1]

Because medical tests, drugs, and treatments can be patented, companies that develop genetic tests can profit from those procedures. Just as pharmaceutical companies have patents on medicines, biogenetic companies can file for patents on genetic tests. Some companies even patent sections of the human genome, claiming that they have spent millions of dollars discovering genes and gene fragments and therefore have a right to profit from their discoveries. This allows them to have some control over any tests, procedures, or drugs that result from that genetic information.

Privately held drug companies are at odds with the Human Genome Project, which is publicly funded and whose findings are freely available to everyone. The amount of money at stake amounts to billions of dollars. The day before the Celera Genomics Group, a privately held biotechnology company, announced that it had completed a rough draft of the human genome, stock in the company jumped 50 percent. The day of the announcement the stock leaped another 26 percent, because many people recognized the potential for biogenetics and wanted to own a piece of the action.

But the day after President Clinton publicly stated, "We've got to get the basic information out to everybody who might find some particular use for it,"[2] the price of Celera's stock fell sharply. In a single day, the stock price fell lower than it had been for months, because people were worried that the government might interfere with Celera's ownership of genetic information.

The issue is far from resolved. With so much money at stake, scientists, academics, government officials, and private industry will probably be fighting over rights to information about the human genetic code for decades.

Animals can be genetically engineered to resist disease.

Genetic Engineering and DNA-Based Products

There are already many DNA-based products on the market. With the increased understanding of genetics that will follow the completion of the Human Genome Project, we can expect thousands more.

Most of the available products are for plants and animals. Companies manufacture a variety of DNA-based products that can diagnose diseases, stimulate growth, and increase the production of products beneficial to people. For example, Prosilac is a vaccine that increases the amount of milk cows produce, and Rabora is a vaccine that helps to control rabies in wild animal populations.

There are also products that reduce an animal's susceptibility to fleas. Some products make animals grow larger and healthier so that they produce more meat for human consumption. Some products protect plants from infestation and disease so farmers can yield larger and healthier crops. There are even products that help plants produce vegetables and fruits that do not spoil as rapidly.

In addition to developing vaccines or genetic treatments, genetic scientists can also produce genetically altered plants and animals. For example, it is possible to genetically alter coffee bean plants so that they produce beans with reduced levels of caffeine.

The U.S. Supreme Court in 1980 ruled that "a live, human-made micro-organism is patentable."[3] That ruling meant that companies could develop new types of plants and animals and market them as products. These plants and animals are referred to as "genetically engineered." When scientists genetically engineer plants or animals, they take part of the DNA of one animal or plant and insert it into the DNA of another plant or animal. They use chemicals to cut a section of DNA from a plant or animal with the characteristics they want, such as long life or resistance to a particular disease, and then they splice that section of DNA into the DNA of other plants or animals. This process is called gene-splicing.

One company that markets genetically engineered products is Monsanto. Monsanto produces corn, cotton, canola, and soybean seeds that grow plants resistant to pesticides. "Roundup Ready" seeds

(Monsanto's name for these genetically engineered seeds) are resistant to glyphosate, a herbicide that usually kills both plants and weeds. Plants grown from Roundup Ready seeds do not die when sprayed with glyphosate, so farmers can spray their crops to kill off weeds without endangering their plants. Monsanto, who owns patents on their Roundup Ready seeds, sells both the seeds and the herbicide.

Seeds are also engineered to protect crops from insects. For example, there is a type of bacteria found in soil that kills certain insects; it is called *Bacillus thuringiensis,* or Bt for short. (The toxin is harmful only to insects, not to people or other animals.) Four biotechnology companies (Monsanto, Dow, Novartis, and AgrEvo) have spliced DNA from the Bt bacteria into the DNA of seeds for plants such as corn, soybeans, and potatoes. The result is a genetically engineered seed that yields crops resistant to some insects. If insects try to eat the crops, they die. The use of Bt seed is already widespread. Environmental Media Services, a nonprofit organization, reported that in 1999 about 25 percent of all corn and about 35 percent of soybeans in the United States were grown from Bt seed.[4]

But not everyone is happy about genetically engineered foods. Many groups have formed in the last ten years to warn people of the potential dangers of these altered foods. Part of the problem is that there is currently no way to tell which foods in the grocery store have been genetically engineered. When shoppers buy potatoes, they have no way of knowing if

Some companies already market genetically engineered corn, cotton, canola, and soybean seeds that grow plants resistant to pesticides.

those potatoes have been genetically altered. They might be buying potatoes engineered to contain pesticides, such as Bt.

Many of the groups opposed to genetically engineered foods recommend the labeling of these foods so that they are more easily identified and avoided. But governmental agencies in the United States have been slow to respond to their requests. One of the reasons is because no one is sure which agency has the authority to regulate these foods. The Food and Drug Administration (FDA), which is responsible for the regulation of the food industries, claims that because the potatoes contain pesticides, the FDA has no authority to regulate their production and distribution. It claims that pesticidal foods are the responsibility of the Environmental Protection Agency (EPA). But the EPA claims that products such as genetically engineered potatoes are food and therefore the responsibility of the FDA.

Monsanto, which produces potatoes genetically engineered to contain pesticides, claims that they "should not have to vouchsafe the safety of biotech food. Our interest," a spokesperson for the company explains, "is selling as much of it as possible. Assuring its safety is the FDA's job."[5]

Monsanto has also engineered into some of its seeds something called "terminator" technology. Terminator crops and plants are sterile and do not produce seeds or flowers. This prevents farmers from reusing seeds and protects Monsanto's investment. Although some view this as a reasonable business practice for Monsanto, others complain that it could make life very difficult for poor farmers (who produce as much as 20 percent of the world's food supply), since they cannot afford to buy new seed every year.[6] The same groups that oppose foods genetically engineered to contain pesticides also strongly oppose the use of terminator technology. These groups fear that terminator technology may spread, resulting in the death of many insects, birds, and animals that rely on plants for survival. Terminator technology could, some argue, result in large regions of essentially lifeless lands.

Gene technology can produce vegetables with more vitamins, larger trees, longer lived plants, seedless oranges, and disease-resistant wheat, but farmers around the world are still torn over the issue of planting genetically altered seed. Although the seed allows them to increase the yield of their crops and lessen spoilage, they face a market that is increasingly more nervous about the new genetically engineered foods. Japan and much of Europe have already made it clear that they are reluctant to embrace these new foods.

It is impossible to predict the price the environment may pay for sweeter corn, richer tea, redder tomatoes, and fatter cows. But one thing is certain: The heated debate between companies that stand to profit from new, genetically engineered products and people who use those products will continue well into this century.

DNA-Based Technologies

Of the many advances we can expect as a result of the Human Genome Project, not all involve the engineering of new genetic codes. Because of the size of the project, many technological advances are being developed to aid in the analysis of genetic materials. Engineers are creating new computer hardware and software that can analyze data more quickly and are designing smaller and smaller computers to handle the massive amount of data on the human genome.

What shape these new technologies will take remains to be seen, but there is a lot of guessing

Genetically engineered seeds help farmers grow larger and healthier crops.

going on. What we do know is that whatever emerges from the project will be faster, smaller, and less expensive than the technology we currently have.

The National Institute for Standards and Technology (NIST) predicts that "the availability of technology which provides cost-efficient, sequence-based analysis of that code will affect virtually all industries that currently rely upon or service biological organisms."[7] Over the next few decades, it will become easier for industries to get and use information about DNA in plants and animals. In the medical field, it may soon be possible for a physician to take a biological sample (such as a mole), inject it into a small cartridge, have a computer automatically perform an accurate analysis of the sample, display the results on a computer screen, and then transfer the data to the patient's computerized record.

Industries working with agriculture and the environment will also benefit. NIST envisions that small, portable hand-held devices will become available that will make it possible for scientists, researchers, and farmers to sequence and analyze DNA while they are walking through crops or nature preserves. It may even become possible to carefully track how environmental conditions, such as shifts in weather, create mutations in plants and animals.

Because of the increased efficiency of new DNA technologies, the cost of having analysis completed on a DNA sample could be reduced by as much as 99 percent. The reduced cost of devices designed to analyze DNA could make analysis readily available to industries that now must send samples to a genetic lab for analysis.

Like other technological advances, such as the personal computer and compact disk players, the less expensive DNA-based technologies are, the more widespread they will become. You may one day be able to input a sample of your DNA from a strand of your hair into your home computer, link to an Internet database, and complete a sophisticated analysis of your genetic history, complete with the names and addresses of distant relatives around the world.

Benefits to Science: Bioarchaeology

Archaeology is the study of the physical remains of a civilization. Archaeologists examine the buildings and artifacts of an area's previous inhabitants and make informed guesses about how those people lived. Bioarchaeology is a relatively new field of study, which began in the early 1980s with a group of young scientists who all shared a similar interest in the human remains of past civilizations. Clark Larsen, one of the founders of bioarchaeology and a professor of anthropology at the University of North Carolina at Chapel Hill, defines bioarchaeology as "the study of the human biological component of the archaeological record."[8]

Instead of examining ruins and broken pottery, bioarchaeologists study human remains, such as teeth and bone fragments. Bioarchaeologists may use electron microscopes to scan the surface of teeth for patterns left in the bone by seeds and specific types of foods, or they may use mass spectrometers to analyze the chemical content of bones and thereby identify particular foods that the person ate when he or she was alive.

Bioarchaeologists can tell a great deal from the bones of people who lived hundreds of years ago. Many foods, such as corn and shellfish, leave chemical signatures in the bone. By tracking the presence or absence of such chemical signatures in bones from different periods, bioarchaeologists can trace the overall eating habits of an entire civilization.

The shape of bones is determined in part by the

amount of weight those bones had to endure over the course of a human lifetime. Bioarchaeologists can determine a great deal about the types of work a civilization engaged in by the shape of the bones. Clark Larsen says, "The skeleton is a wonderfully informative record of a person's lifetime. . . . It's a . . . picture of what that person did with their life."[9]

Once the human genome is mapped and scientists begin to reveal its secrets, bioarchaeologists will no longer have to rely on observation. They will be able to map the genetic makeup of the bones left behind by civilizations, and from those bones they will be able to reconstruct the lineage and development of entire groups of people. DNA analysis will take much of the guesswork out of understanding past civilizations.

Benefits to Science: Anthropology

Anthropology is the study of human beings: their cultures, their beliefs, their customs, their relationships, and their physical development. Having a complete map of the human genome will make it possible for anthropologists to trace the relationships between people and cultures.

One important question that anthropologists examine is where human beings originated and when they moved from place to place. And advances in our understanding of human DNA have already helped us get a clearer understanding of our heritage.

For example, researchers from Sweden and Germany recently selected DNA samples from fifty-three people from different parts of the world. These researchers used technologies developed by the Human Genome Project to examine and compare 16,500 base pairs from these subjects. Their findings indicate that the genetic makeup of Africans is "twice as diverse" as that of other nationalities. This means that Africans have the oldest DNA of the groups studied.

From their findings, the Swedish and German researchers concluded that:

- All human beings originated in Africa.

- Modern human beings left Africa as recently as fifty thousand years ago (it was previously thought that our ancestors migrated out of Africa one hundred thousand years ago).

- The number of human beings on the planet increased substantially around thirty-eight thousand years ago.

- A common ancestor of all human beings may have lived 170,000 years ago.

Ulf Gyllensten, a geneticist and the chief researcher involved in the study, says, "There was probably a fairly small group that migrated out of Africa and that population probably spread in several directions and grew pretty quickly."[10]

Genetics can lead to startling discoveries about our history. One study by Mark Seielstad of the Harvard School of Public Health examined the DNA of women and men and discovered that women's genes appeared very well mixed. Men's genes were less mixed. This implies that the genetic code of

Anthropologists have found that Africans have the most diverse DNA of all the groups studied. Shown are a Masai mother and child from Kenya.

women might actually carry more geographic diversity than the genetic code of men. These results suggest that women actually traveled the world more than men, despite the fact that most history books present men as the world travelers. Seielstad says that one possible explanation for these findings is that when men and women married, it was often the women who moved.[11]

Although the findings of these researchers are not conclusive, and some question the accuracy of the methods they used, they do indicate the importance of understanding the human genome to the understanding of human origins. Once an accurate map of the human genome has been thoroughly studied, it may be possible to trace the entire history of human beings through genetic code, providing us with insight into the course of human development.

6

Social Issues

"Today we are learning the language in which God created life," President Clinton said of the Human Genome Project.[1] He was not overstating the matter. In mapping our own genetic code, we shed light on thousands of issues that have remained in darkness as long as we have been around. The Human Genome Project may eventually have more effect on how we live and deal with each other than any earlier scientific advance.

Little was publicly known about individuals at the end of the twentieth century. If you were a detective and were willing to invest a lot of time, you could probably uncover some basic information, such as someone's full name, address, social security number, driver's license number, and the schools he or she attended. But there was little you could actually ascertain about people themselves. What were the chances someone would develop a debilitating disease? How smart were they? How physically fit?

Nearly all personal information about people was based on evaluation and guesswork: test scores, past performance, your impressions when you met them. If they earned low scores in school, you might assume they were not particularly intelligent. But that is not a foolproof system. Albert Einstein, one of the greatest mathematicians of the twentieth century and the man who came up with the theory of relativity, failed math in grade school. Bill Gates, who created the Microsoft computer company and became the wealthiest person alive, dropped out of college. Even Charles Darwin did poorly in grade school. So we may think we know how intelligent people are, but miss the mark by quite a bit.

The same is true for physical health. Someone who looks healthy, eats right, and gets plenty of exercise may die at a young age, while someone who is overweight, eats junk food, smokes cigarettes, and never exercises may live to be eighty. Consider Jim Fixx, the long-distance runner who did much to launch the American fitness revolution in the 1970s. Fixx died of a heart attack at the age of fifty-two while running, despite his apparent good health. It was a big surprise to many.

The mapping of the human genome promises to take much of the guesswork out of the evaluation of human potential. At first glance, this may seem like an undeniably important advance, but it has many people very worried. What happens when a complete record of your genetic makeup exists? Who gets access to it? What decisions will they make based on that information? These are some of the questions the Human Genome Project is addressing.

Fair Use of Genetic Information

The Ethical, Legal, and Social Issues Working Group (ELSI) of the National Action Plan on Breast Cancer (NAPBC) argues that state and federal governments must be careful to regulate how employers use genetic information when making decisions about employees. One of the recommendations that the NAPBC-ELSI has made to federal and state policy makers is that employers be "prohibited from using genetic information to affect the hiring of an individual or to affect the terms, conditions, privileges, benefits, or termination of employment unless the employment organization can prove this information is job related and consistent with business activity."[2] Their concern is that once detailed genetic information is available, employers will use that information to deny basic rights to individual employees.

Currently there is no national legislation restricting an employer's access to genetic information about its employees or preventing employers or insurance companies from using genetic information to deny people work or coverage. But the increase in our knowledge of genetics is relatively recent, and the amount of genetic information about individuals that is now available is extremely limited. What happens when a genetic blueprint is available for all employees? Should employers have the right to refuse employment to potential employees based on information contained in their genetic code? If two people with equal qualifications apply for a position with an employer, and one of the applicants has a genetic predisposition for a major medical condition, such as heart disease or Alzheimer's, should the employer be allowed to hire the candidate with the more favorable genetic code?

Questions such as these are not as easy as they may first appear. Remember, not all people with the genes for a particular disease will get that disease. An 85 percent chance of contracting a disease during your lifetime leaves a 15 percent chance that you will remain healthy. Should you be sent to the unemployment line simply because you *might* develop a life-threatening disease? And if people with unfavorable genes cannot get jobs, who will support them? Will the government pay to keep them fed and sheltered?

State Senator Dianne Byrum has already introduced legislation that would guard the people of Michigan from discrimination based on genetic information. Byrum believes that "if an employer knows

the diseases you're likely to have, given the compet-
itiveness of the job market, they may not choose
you."[3] According to Edward Goldman, a legal expert
for the University of Michigan Health System, a few
employers already have tried using genetic information to screen prospective employees.[4]

One reason employers may want to use genetic
information to deny certain applicants employment is
because of insurance rates. Insurance company rates
are based on actuarial tables, mathematical estimates
of the likelihood that someone will develop a serious
illness or die. These estimates are based on nonper-
sonal data, such as the region of the country the
person lives in. People in large cities, for example,
have a much higher chance of contracting breathing
ailments. Therefore, insurance companies charge
higher rates to insure people in cities than they do in
small towns, where air pollution is at a minimum.

But when detailed genetic information is available, insurance companies would be able to pinpoint
specific people with a higher risk for disease. They
could decide to charge higher premiums to those
people. Because employers usually pay the bulk of
health insurance premiums for their employees, they
would face a higher financial burden if they hired
people who were genetically predisposed to contract
diseases. Worse yet, insurance companies could
refuse to insure them at all.

The simple economics of the issue is that illness
in the workforce costs employers a great deal of
money. They not only face greater insurance rates,

but they also have to replace workers who are out ill. ELSI is already examining these issues and points out that employers and insurance companies have plenty of reasons to want "to screen workers."[5] But screening workers and potential employees, many people warn, could result in a genetic class system. Those with desirable genes would have a great many opportunities for prosperity and personal satisfaction, which would be denied people with undesirable genes.

Privacy, Confidentiality, and Genetic Information as Product

Do people own their own genetic codes, and do they have the right to restrict access to information contained in their DNA? This is one of the most important questions that people will have to solve in the near future. Many organizations are already busy trying to limit access to genetic information in order to preserve what they view as a critical human right—the right to control how one's own genetic information is used and disseminated.

On February 8, 2000, President Clinton issued an executive order banning genetic discrimination throughout the federal government. The order protects the following genetic information:

- information about an individual's genetic tests;

- information about the genetic tests of an individual's family members; or

President Bill Clinton issued an executive order on February 8, 2000, banning genetic discrimination throughout the federal government.

- information about the occurrence of a disease, medical condition, or disorder in family members of the individual.[6]

The issue may seem simple—no one should have access to genetic information about us without our consent. But the issue is much more complicated than that. Because virtually every cell in our body contains a complete copy of our DNA, the basic sample needed to extract that information is easy to acquire. Every time you shed skin cells, you leave behind a copy of your genetic code, and people shed millions of skin cells. These cells are falling off us around the clock as new cells replace them. About once a month, a person grows a completely new covering of skin, while last month's skin is scattered everywhere: in bedsheets, in the shower, in the car, in our clothes. Every place we go, we leave skin cells behind.

And there are issues more significant than mere accessibility. David Korn, a professor of pathology at Stanford University School of Medicine, points out that medical researchers and physicians routinely use samples of human tissue for study, review, and the training of new physicians. Currently, the use of these samples only requires "minimal informed consent" because such use poses "'minimal risk' to patient sources and does not 'adversely affect [their] rights and welfare.'"[7] But, Korn goes on to say,

> the advent of these new genetic research techniques . . . has changed the calculus of risk. In the course of their studies, researchers may discover information that could profoundly affect the lives of the tissue sources and even their relatives.[8]

Most hospitals and university medical centers contain large archives of human tissue samples. If strict regulations are passed regarding the use of human tissue samples, physicians and scientists could have a difficult time obtaining much-needed specimens. This could slow down some medical advances.

One bill drafted to protect individual rights regarding genetic information—the Genetic Privacy Act (which was drafted by George J. Annas, Leonard

H. Glantz, and Patricia A. Roche of the Health Law Department of Boston University School of Public Health)—is particularly strict. Before a DNA sample can be taken, the person—or, as the document refers to him or her, the "sample source"—must be informed of all of the following:

1. that consent to the collection or taking of the DNA sample is voluntary;

2. that consent to the genetic analysis is voluntary;

3. of the information that can reasonably be expected to be derived from the genetic analysis;

4. of the use, if any, that the sample source or the sample source's representative will be able to make of the information derived from the genetic analysis;

5. of the right to inspect records that contain information derived from the genetic analysis;

6. of the right to have the DNA sample destroyed;

7. of the right to revoke consent to the genetic analysis at any time prior to the completion of the analysis;

8. that the genetic analysis may result in information about the sample source's genetic relatives which may not be known to such relatives but could be important, and if so the sample source will have to decide whether or not to share that information with relatives;

9. that in the future someone else may ask if the sample source has obtained genetic testing or analysis and condition a benefit on the disclosure of information regarding such testing or analysis;

10. that the collection and analysis of the DNA sample, and the private genetic information derived from the analysis is protected by this Act; and

11. of the availability of genetic counseling.[9]

Korn calls the Genetic Privacy Act one of the "most extreme" of the documents being circulated.[10] He points out that many times when a pathologist performs an initial examination of a sample, the results of that examination "indicate the need for additional diagnostic tests."[11] Many of these tests would meet the definition for genetic tests. Under the guidelines put forth by the Genetic Privacy Act, a "pathologist would have to return to the patient to obtain specific informed consent before performing each of the tests in the diagnostic sequence."[12]

Some states, such as Oregon and New Jersey, have already passed Genetic Privacy Acts at the state level. How the national government will protect the rights of citizens is still in question, but many feel that some protection must be offered. Already organizations have begun to use genetic information without the consent of the people from whom that information was harvested. For example, Boston University recently entered into a for-profit arrangement with investors to form Framingham Genomic

Medicine, Inc. The new company was to provide a database on "genetic, clinical, and behavioral data"[13] collected over fifty years from more than ten thousand heart attack and stroke patients. This was done without the consent of these patients.

There was also an issue of access. Various organizations and government agencies complained about the venture because many of them had donated money to the Framingham Heart Study and expected that information to remain freely available to the public. Unable to resolve conflicts of interest, Boston University abandoned its efforts to start the company. In this case, the problem was solved without a law on the books, but will future companies be as cooperative as Framingham Genomic Medicine, Inc.?

In the new age of genetics, genetic information is valuable. Although the original aim of the Human Genome Project was to map the human genome for the good of humanity, many companies and organizations have already begun seeing a lot of money in those strings of DNA. The biggest player in the genetic gold rush is Celera Genomics Group, the privately held biotechnology company that claimed victory in the race to map the human genome. J. Craig Venter, the director of Celera, said of the completion of the draft that the human race could now "read the letters of its own text."[14] But not without a price.

Celera is interested in profit and vigorously pursues private patents on every fragment of the genome that it maps. Some people complain that Celera made extensive use of the public databases made freely available to all interested parties by the public project, yet it carefully guarded all of its advances.

Celera's result will eventually be made available, but "the company will claim royalties from any commercial pharmaceutical application of its discoveries."[15] Many people, even in the biotech industry, are against the private ownership of any part of the human genome. These people consider Celera's attempt to claim ownership and control over DNA sequences very bad.

Reproductive Issues

The existence of a complete copy of the human genome will drastically alter the way people reproduce. One hundred years ago, the only defense a couple with family histories of genetic disorders had against the possibility of giving birth to children with birth defects was to avoid having children. Genetics offers them other alternatives.

It is already possible for parents to determine if a fetus carries some genetic disorders. If an analysis of a fetus's DNA indicates that the unborn child has a genetic disorder, parents can choose to continue with the birth or terminate the pregnancy. The more knowledge we gain about the structure of human genetic code, the more physicians and medical technicians will be able to tell about a child before he or she is born. This concerns many people who fear that parents will not restrict their decision to abort or continue a pregnancy to serious genetic disorders.

They worry that parents who want a boy may choose to terminate the pregnancy if they discover the fetus is a girl. But what happens if it becomes possible for parents to determine other characteristics about their unborn offspring, such as intelligence or hair color? Should parents have the right to choose the characteristics of their offspring? What happens if genetic tests determine that an unborn child, if carried to term, will have average intelligence? Should parents be allowed to terminate the pregnancy and try again, or should there be regulations limiting the rights of parents?

The more we learn about the human genome, the more complicated this issue will become. That is because it is not only possible but likely that we will soon have the knowledge and the technology to allow parents to alter the DNA of their children while they are still in the womb.

There are two ways that the DNA of a fetus can be altered:

1. Somatic cell gene modification: the modification of "differentiated" body cells, such as muscle, blood, or liver cells, after fertilization occurs.

2. Germ line gene modification: the modification of the "undifferentiated" cells of an early embryo, or of sperm or egg cells before fertilization occurs.

Somatic cell gene modification will only affect the biological development of the organism on which it is performed. For example, if we alter the somatic cells of a cow embryo so that it will produce more milk when it is born, only that cow will produce more milk. Descendants of that cow will not carry the gene for increased milk production. If we perform germ line gene modification on the cow when it is a new embryo or perform modification on the sperm or egg used to conceive the cow, then that cow and all generations of that cow will carry the gene for increased milk production.[16]

The idea that we might prevent offspring from developing diseases and physical deformities is inviting. If you could do something to prevent your children from harmful physical ailments, would you?

Germ line modification results in traits—such as increased milk production among cows—that are passed down from one generation to another.

Even if it meant tampering with their DNA? If we choose to eliminate physical ailments from our children, why not our children's children and our children's children's children? Why not simply wipe out physical problems for all future generations?

Why not go further—rather than just eliminating genes that carry unfavorable physical characteristics, why not use germ line gene modification to improve our genetic line? Daniel E. Koshland, Jr., editor-in-chief of *Science* and a molecular biologist himself, acknowledges that germ line modification could be seen as a way of making people "better at computers, better as musicians, [and] better physically."[17]

It is only a matter of time before we have the knowledge and technology to perform germ line gene modification on people. But should we just because we can? Many groups do not think so. The Council for Responsible Genetics, for example, voices several objections to germ line gene modification.

1. It is not needed to save the lives or alleviate the suffering of existing people, because its target population is "future people" who have not yet even been conceived.

2. It is bad for society to treat people as flawed objects. People who fall short of some technically achievable ideal would increasingly be seen as "damaged goods." And it is clear that the standards for what is genetically desirable will be those of the society's economically and politically dominant groups. This will only reinforce prejudices and discrimination in a society where they already exist.

3. In the future, people who suffer physically or emotionally as a result of earlier germ line modifications would have no way to hold the people responsible accountable for the harm caused them.[18]

Despite these concerns, many people look forward to the day when molecular science will make it possible to improve future generations. They see human genetic modification as a powerful step toward the inevitable improvement of the human race. Others see it as a return to eugenics and fear that tampering with human DNA will result in class divisions between those with medically improved genes and those who either choose not to alter their family's gene pool or cannot afford genetic procedures.

Psychological Effects

We may not be able to predict exactly how the public will react once genetic testing is in widespread use, but we can be certain that they will react. When information is available about which diseases and disorders people carry in their genes, some people are bound to suffer.

Some groups of people are at high risk for some diseases. Central European Jews, for example, are ten times as likely as other people to contract Tay-Sachs syndrome. Tay-Sachs syndrome is a deadly brain disease that usually results in a painful death by the age of three or four. Understandably, families would prefer to avoid going through the pain and hardship of having a child with the syndrome. One way people have tried to assure that the disease is not passed on is to have premarital genetic tests performed to determine if both the man and woman are carrying the allele for Tay-Sachs. If the trait is found, the wedding is sometimes called off.[19]

This type of testing may seem beneficial, but what is the psychological impact on someone who learns he or she is a carrier? Imagine the trauma of having your wedding canceled and having other people in your tight-knit community know that you carry an undesirable trait in your genetic code.

Knowing what is in our genes may result in some people being stigmatized. People may be shunned or ostracized by their culture, community, or family based on what is in their genes, leaving them feeling outcast, alone, alienated, and inferior. Darryl Macer argues that "it may not be in the best interest to know all the genetic traits that we or a fetus possess."[20]

If the past is any indication, we will not be able to avoid genetic discrimination, but we may limit the severity of that discrimination through educational programs, public awareness campaigns, and open discussions.

7

Legal and Ethical Issues

The Human Genome Project may ultimately lead to drastic changes in the way we live. Some people welcome these changes, seeing them as signs of human progress. Others are concerned about the effect such changes might have on our legal system and how they might alter existing attitudes about right and wrong.

Legal Issues

The Human Genome Project and the advances in our understanding of genetics have already had an impact on our legal system. In 1980, the U.S. Supreme Court

86

ruled that a genetically altered life form could be patented.[1] This meant that scientists could own the new life forms they developed.

Laws have also been passed to prevent the federal government from discriminating against employees based on genetic information and to prevent health providers from increasing rates for federal employees based on "predictive genetic information."[2] Many more laws will be passed as the Human Genome Project is completed and we move into what many are calling the age of biotechnology.

In 1980, the U.S. Supreme Court had to decide if genetically altered life forms could be patented. The Court will face even more difficult issues in the next hundred years as a result of the Human Genome Project.

Florida v. *Andrews* was the first legal case to use DNA to obtain a conviction. Based on genetic evidence, the defendant was convicted of twenty cases of sexual and attempted sexual assault. With this case, the Florida District Court of Appeal established that "'genetic fingerprint' evidence was admissible."[3] Since then, DNA evidence has become commonplace in the courtroom.

There are two types of legal evidence: circumstantial and physical. Circumstantial evidence consists of items such as eyewitness reports, documents, and records. Physical evidence consists of actual physical objects such as bloodstains or a murder weapon. Of the two types, physical evidence carries the most weight in a court of law.

Genetics offers some of the most accurate physical evidence available to the legal system. The legal system already uses DNA fingerprinting because DNA is unique to each individual (except in the case of identical twins), and therefore is an excellent way of determining the source of a biological sample (such as a drop of blood at a crime scene). Eric Lander, the director of the MIT Center for Genome Research, claims that DNA fingerprinting has made a "major contribution . . . to the criminal justice system."[4] In many cases, DNA evidence helps prosecutors to "conclusively establish the guilt of a defendant."[5]

The trial of O. J. Simpson was one of the most famous trials of the twentieth century. The football star was accused of murdering his ex-wife, Nicole

Brown Simpson, and Ronald Goldman, one of her friends. The prosecutors in the case relied heavily on the DNA testing of blood found at the crime scene, in O. J. Simpson's automobile, in his ex-wife's house, and on a pair of socks and a single glove. A total of forty-five drops of blood were analyzed. The DNA tests linked all forty-five to either O. J. Simpson, his ex-wife, or her friend. The glove had blood from all three, and so became a key piece of evidence. The prosecutors in the case were unable to convince the jury that the glove belonged to Simpson, and Simpson was eventually acquitted and freed, but a later civil lawsuit found Simpson guilty in the double homicide. The civil court ordered Simpson to pay $33.5 million in damages, but Simpson remained free.

Most criminals confess when confronted with DNA evidence linking them to a crime, which speeds justice and saves taxpayers the expense of a trial. DNA fingerprinting has helped to convict hundreds of perpetrators of violent crime. But DNA finger-printing is not just about convicting the guilty. A 1996 study by the government studied twenty-eight sexual-assault cases that were reversed based on DNA testing. DNA evidence helped to free the twenty-eight defendants, but only after they had served a combined total of 127 years for crimes they did not commit.

Former Attorney General Janet Reno pointed out that "the use of forensic science as a tool in the search for truth allows justice to be done not only by apprehending the guilty but also by freeing the innocent."[6] Our knowledge of DNA has helped the justice system convict many criminals who would otherwise have gone undetected and free many people wrongly accused of crimes.

Despite the value of DNA fingerprinting, it is still only 95–99 percent accurate. But in the wake of the Human Genome Project, even more accurate, less expensive genetic tests will be devised. Information about the human genome should eventually allow geneticists to determine hair color, height, race, eye color, health conditions, and hundreds of other details, all from something as minute as a speck of

New techniques for mapping DNA will make it easier for organizations such as the FBI to capture and convict lawbreakers. Shown is the gangster Al Capone.

dandruff. It should soon be possible to match the suspect to the sample with near 100 percent certainty.

Constitutional Protection

Americans do not have to worry about patents on genetically altered people. Although there are no laws that explicitly state that you cannot patent people who have had their genetic code changed, the United States Patent Office and official government policy forbid the patenting of human beings. In addition, section one of the thirteenth amendment to the United States Constitution states: "Neither slavery nor involuntary servitude, except as a punishment for crime whereof the party shall have been duly convicted, shall exist within the United States, or any place subject to their jurisdiction."[7] If someone were allowed to patent a human being, that would qualify as slavery, because a patent represents ownership. The human being's DNA, thus the human being, would belong to the patent holder. It is therefore prohibited by this amendment.

Also of importance to genetic legal issues is Title VII of the Civil Rights Act of 1964. Title VII protects people from job discrimination based on "race, color, religion, sex, or national origin."[8] Because race and sex are genetically determined, they can be associated with genetic predispositions to some diseases; therefore, the Civil Rights Act offers some protection from discrimination based on genetic information, mainly protection for those genetic predispositions that can be linked to sex or race.

Some people believe that they are also protected by a constitutional right to privacy against unauthorized access to genetic information. But the Constitution is not explicit about rights of privacy. There have been many cases where the first, the fourth, and the fifth amendments have been used to justify protection. The first amendment guarantees freedoms of religion, speech, assembly, and the press; the fourth amendment guarantees protection against unreasonable search and seizure; and the fifth amendment guarantees civil and criminal rights. The Supreme Court used these amendments to justify their 1967 ruling that outlawed wiretapping. But there have also been cases where the courts ruled that some information about a person was not protected. In 1974 the Supreme Court ruled that bank records were the property of the bank. This means that a bank could legally track the spending habits of their clients, if they were so inclined.

How will it all play out once the Human Genome Project is complete and it becomes possible to obtain a complete genetic record of a person? Once that information exists, there are bound to be individuals and organizations that misuse that information. In the next hundred years, the Supreme Court will find itself addressing many difficult questions.

People who have a genetic predisposition for a disease may be able to seek protection from discrimination under the 1990 Americans with Disabilities Act (ADA). In 1995, the Equal Employment Opportunities Commission extended protection under the disabilities act to include "individuals who experience employment discrimination based on genetic information related to illness, disease, or other disorders."[9]

Despite these protections, existing laws are not enough to ensure that scientific advances in the field of genetics do not threaten the individual human rights of citizens. New laws will have to be drafted, and the drafting of these laws will be accompanied by heated debate.

Ethical Issues

The field of ethics is concerned with issues of right and wrong. Most of us learned our ideas about right and wrong from our parents when we were growing up. Because we develop our notions of right and wrong—our ethical ideas—when we are very young, we sometimes sense that they are (or should be) true for everyone. When it seems obvious to us that something is wrong, we may wonder why everyone does not see it the same way.

Theories about ethics formally originate with the early Greek philosophers. Socrates (circa 469–399 B.C.) was one of the first people to write about ethics. He felt that each person had a soul and that if a person examined the world around him, he or she would come to understand what is true and right, because what is true and right is not exclusive to one person, but is true and right for everyone.

But Socrates' view is not the only view of ethics. There have been dozens of other major theories.

Some are based on feeling ("I *feel* that this is wrong"); some are based on reason ("I *think* that this is wrong"). For example, Jeremy Bentham (1748–1832) and John Stuart Mill (1806–1873) helped to form the philosophical school of utilitarianism. In his 1789 book, *Introduction to the Principles of Morals and Legislation,* Bentham argued that whatever produces the most happiness is right. Utilitarianism has often been characterized as a philosophy that promotes the greatest good for the greatest number. To a utilitarian, what is right and ethical is whatever results in the most happiness for the largest number of people.

Whether or not people consider the Human Genome Project and the many social changes that accompany it to be ethical depends on what their ethical views are. Someone may, if he or she agrees with Socrates that right and wrong are constant, believe that it is wrong to alter the natural genetic code of living things. Someone else, who sides more with Jeremy Bentham and the utilitarians, may reach the conclusion that if experimenting with our DNA can cure cancer, sickle-cell anemia, hemophilia, and hundreds of other human ailments, it must be right.

ELSI and the Human Genome Project

ELSI stands for Ethical, Legal, and Social Issues, and it is an integral part of the Human Genome Project. From the start, researchers have been aware of the broad impact the project could have on every facet of human life. From the beginning of the project, researchers have been developing "guidelines and frameworks for ensuring the safe and appropriate use of genetic information [that] are crucial to the success of the Human Genome Project."[10]

ELSI is divided into four program areas.

1. Privacy and Fairness in the Use and Interpretation of Genetic Information:

   Researchers working in this area look into issues involving the use and distribution of genetic information. As more genetic information about people becomes available, who has access to that information and how that information is used is vitally important. One of ELSI's goals is to make sure that procedures and guidelines are in place when society reaches the point where genetic information might be used to discriminate against individuals who carry genes for certain disorders. What constitutes "fair use" of genetic information for employers, the military, adoption agencies, insurance companies, and the criminal justice system?

   This program area also deals with how families, social groups, and individuals might react to genetic information about themselves or someone they know. What will be the psychological impact of genetic information? And what philosophical changes will people undergo regarding their sense of individuality?

2. Clinical Integration of New Genetic Technologies:

   The second program area of ELSI is primarily concerned with genetic counseling. How should genetic information be delivered to patients? What information should be delivered? How will this information be explained to people who are planning to have children?

   The program area also looks into cultural differences and how access to genetic information and genetic testing may be denied to people of differing cultural backgrounds. For example, would some cultures have limited access because they are poorer than others?

3. Issues Surrounding Genetic Research:

   The third program area of ELSI investigates procedures and methods for protecting the privacy of individuals and providing safeguards to prevent genetic information from being released to the wrong people or at an inappropriate time. The area deals with issues regarding patient confidentiality and issues related to the commercialization of biological samples used in genetic research.

4. Public and Professional Education:

   New information that surfaces from the Human Genome Project will change the way many people go about their occupations and

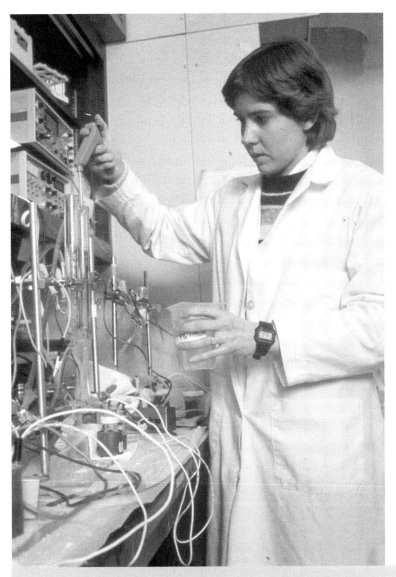

One concern about genetic research is that information about people's predisposition to certain diseases might be used to discriminate against them. For this reason, researchers must be careful to safeguard people's privacy.

lives. Yet most people know very little about genetics.

Certainly it is important for health care providers to have a good understanding of genetics and the role genes play in health, but it is important for the general public to have a basic understanding of genetics too. The world in which we all live is changing, and it is vital that we understand those changes.

A portion of the research ELSI funds examines methods for teaching professionals and the public about genetics in order to best prepare people for the difficult decisions they will have to make in the next one hundred years.[11]

How will society react to the drastic changes in the next 100–200 years? We can only imagine. But at least the Human Genome Project recognizes that many of these changes will be confusing for people and will challenge some of their most closely held beliefs.

Cosmetic Genetics

One of the most sensitive issues surrounding the Human Genome Project is the question of what people should be allowed to alter once it is possible to alter anything. Most people agree that altering genes to eliminate cancer is morally right. But what about altering genes to make us more attractive? To make us smarter? To make us live longer?

Consider James Watson's far-reaching comments on the future of genetics. Watson says, "We all know how imperfect we are. Why not make ourselves a little better suited for survival? That's what we'll do. We'll make ourselves a little better."[12] But what does it mean to make ourselves better?

Most people agree that saving people from the physical and emotional pain of disease and deformity is a worthy goal, but deciding on what is and what is not a deformity is not a simple matter. If we limit the use of genetic therapy to disorders, we will inevitably create inequity. Consider Catherine Baker's hypothetical example from "Your Genes, Your Choices": Suppose two boys who are about the same age are not growing at a normal rate. Both will end up being just over five feet tall. The first boy is short because he lacks an important growth hormone. The second is short because his parents were short. Should the second boy be denied gene therapy just because his shortness is not the result of a medical condition? Would it be fair to offer treatment to the first and not the second?[13]

The question at the center of Baker's example is, What qualifies as a treatable condition? How do we distinguish between real medical conditions and issues of vanity? Should we limit access to genetic treatments and risk denying one person the same treatment as another, or should we allow people to genetically change any physical trait they want?

As new gene therapies become available, medical health professionals will find themselves facing many of these ethical dilemmas. Is baldness a treatable condition in women, but not in men? If it becomes possible, should we use gene therapy to eliminate bad eyesight? What about skin that is prone to wrinkles?

Today plastic surgery is a $3 billion a year industry. Tens of thousands of people flock to surgeons every year for face-lifts, liposuction, tummy tucks, and other purely cosmetic procedures. Some feel this pursuit of physical beauty is vain and that people should accept the way they look. Others argue that there is nothing wrong with improving yourself by any means available.

Designer Babies

It may be a long time before genetics is able to do a great deal to alter the basic characteristics of adults, but in the very near future geneticists will have the tools necessary to make substantial changes to people before they are born. The more we understand where genes are located in the genome and how they function, the more we will be able to tweak them to produce characteristics we desire.

Within the next one hundred years it should be possible for parents to choose the characteristics of their offspring. They could choose basic physical characteristics such as sex, height, hair and eye color, and they could choose other characteristics such as intelligence, dexterity, athletic ability, and temperament. Would anyone purposefully choose to have a child who was not intelligent? A child who was not physically strong and attractive?

Many people are concerned that if these services are made available, only the wealthiest families will be able to afford them. This could create a genetic class system. Those who can afford to genetically engineer their offspring would have advantages over everyone else—advantages that would make it impossible for children who were not genetically engineered to compete.

Choice vs. Chance

The question of whether or not it is right to genetically alter people is ultimately a question of whether people believe in choice or chance. Refusing to improve human beings when we have the technology and knowledge to do so reflects the belief that chance

The difference between human DNA and the DNA of chimpanzees is sometimes less than half of one percent.

is better than choice, the belief that we should let our genes develop on their own. Many people believe that there is a natural order to the world, that however people happen to come together from generation to generation is the way they were *intended* to come together. These people argue that we should not interfere in the natural order of the universe.

Others argue that we should take advantage of every opportunity to improve ourselves. For these people, recent advances in genetics promise us a more active role in the development of the human race. Genetics give us a choice in our future, and people who prefer choice over chance feel that given a choice between brighter, more physically sound people and whatever hodgepodge of DNA chance may generate, it only makes sense to take personal responsibility for humanity's future.

8

A Look to the Future

The Greek philosopher Heraclitus (circa 535–475 B.C.) said nearly twenty-five hundred years ago that the only thing that did not change was the fact that everything changes. In the twenty-first century, we may all see tremendous changes: There will probably be cures for cancer, Alzheimer's disease, and many other genetic disorders. Life expectancy will go up because of a decrease in the number of life-threatening diseases and disorders our DNA will carry from generation to generation. The life span of human beings may also be increased. As soon as the year 2100, people may be living 150–200 years.

With people living longer, we can expect populations to grow substantially, changing the structure of most cultures around the world. The more crowded the planet becomes, the more important it will be to preserve our limited natural resources.

In your lifetime, you may see a world where cloning is as commonplace as surgery. For the most part, cloning will probably be used to perpetuate a desirable genetic code among animals or to grow animals for the purpose of transplanting their healthy organs into human beings whose organs have begun to fail. Some scientists are already working on cloning a human being. Dr. Severino Antinori, a fertility specialist, and Panayiotis M. Zavos, an American scientist, announced on January 25, 2001, that they expect to have cloned human embryos in eighteen to twenty-four months. In defense of the cloning attempt, Zavos said, "The genie is out of the bottle. It's a matter of time when humans will apply it to themselves, and we think this is best initiated by us . . . with ethical guidelines and quality standards."[1]

In November 2001, Advanced Cell Technology, a private company, announced that it had successfully cloned a human embryo. Some questioned the accuracy of the company's claim, arguing that the "embryo" probably would not have grown into a human being. Nevertheless, the announcement caused a flurry of opposition that reached all the way to the Vatican and the White House. President George W. Bush called for legislation banning human cloning on the basis that it is "morally wrong."[2]

Despite these first attempts to clone people, it is unlikely that we will see much human cloning in the immediate future. One roadblock to human cloning is physical defects. There are dozens of failures for

Advances in our understanding of human DNA may soon make it possible to double the human life span.

every successful cloning, even when cloning animals. The second roadblock is the law. Many countries have already begun proposing bans and restrictions on human cloning. On May 3, 2001, the Canadian government proposed legislation banning human cloning. New Zealand's government is considering speeding up the passage of a bill to control genetic changes in reproduction. California, Rhode Island, Louisiana, and Michigan all have state laws against human cloning, and the Texas Legislature just approved a ban on human cloning that calls for penalties of up to $10 million and possible life imprisonment for anyone who tries to clone a human being. In July 2001, the U.S. House of Representatives in a 265–162 vote passed a measure that set fines of $1 million and up to ten years in prison for anyone who clones a human being. Sam Brownback, a senator from Kansas, introduced into the Senate a bill that calls for a ban on all human cloning.

Although we probably will not see much human cloning, it is very likely that people will begin designing the children they want rather than leaving it all up to chance. Undoubtedly, parents will make every effort to improve the chances their children have of a rich and rewarding life. Public opinion and government legislation will limit how much parents are allowed to genetically engineer, but it is almost certain that it will eventually be seen as their right to engineer some qualities.

We can expect genetic testing to become a regular part of our lives, even if we are not in the medical field. Some people argue that better technology will soon make it possible for us to carry around a map of our individual DNA with us. If and when this occurs, we will be able to locate and possibly correct many physical ailments before they have a chance to hurt us.

And there will be many other revolutionary changes. Anthropologists will be better equipped to trace the growth and expansion of the human race. Genealogists will be able to trace family histories much more accurately than they can today. The criminal justice system will have the ability to solve many more crimes, making police work much more effective and providing prosecutors and defense attorneys with invaluable tools for proving the guilt or innocence of defendants.

Once the Human Genome Project is complete, the next step will be to decode what it all means. That could take hundreds of years. Having a complete copy of human DNA is like having a giant book with 3 billion letters all strung together. Before we can read the book, we will have to figure out how those letters go together. But as we decode that great book of human life, we will be unlocking the greatest mystery the human race has ever faced.

Chronology

1859—Charles Darwin publishes *On the Origin of Species*.

1865—Gregor Mendel presents his findings on peas and heredity to the Brünn Natural History Society.

1866—Gregor Mendel publishes his work on peas and inherited traits.

1869—Francis Galton publishes *Hereditary Genius*, in which he concludes that intelligence is passed on through genes.

1884—Cell nucleus is identified as the basis for inheritance.

1888—The word "chromosome" is coined by Heinrich Waldeyer.

1889—Francis Galton publishes *Natural Inheritance*, in which he formulates the "Law of Ancestral Inheritance."

1900—Gregor Mendel's work is finally "discovered" and examined.

1910—Thomas Hunt Morgan discovers that some inherited characteristics are linked to sex.

1937—T. Dobzhansky publishes *Genetics and the Origin of Species.*

1953—Watson and Crick publish their article explaining the double-helix shape of DNA in the journal *Nature.*

1957—A study of peppered moths in England is hailed as an example of natural selection (later found to be flawed).

1962—Watson, Crick, and Wilkins win the Nobel Prize for discovering the structure of DNA.

1990—Human Genome Project begins.

1991—Human Genome Database is established.

1992—Low-resolution linkage map of human genome is published.

1994—Five-year goal of the Human Genome Project is completed (one year early). Genetic Privacy Act is passed.

1995—Sequence of smallest bacterium is completed, along with moderate-resolution maps of human chromosomes 3, 11, 12, and 22 and high-resolution maps of chromosomes 16 and 19. The minimum number of genes needed for independent existence is established.

1998—Department of Energy and National Institutes of Health project that they will be finished sequencing the human genome by 2003.

1999—Human Genome Project predicts it will have a rough draft of entire human genome by

2000. Complete map of chromosome 22 is completed.

2000—National Institutes of Health and Celera Genomics Group announce that a rough draft of the human genome has been completed.

Chapter Notes

Chapter 1. To Know Ourselves

1. Hans Stubbe, *History of Genetics from Prehistoric Times to the Rediscovery of Mendel's Laws,* trans. T.R.W. Waters (Cambridge, Mass.: MIT Press, 1972), p. 16.

2. Euripides, *Phrixus,* Fragment 970. Trans. M. H. Morgan, <http://www.threegraces.com/quotes/e484406.htm> (September 6, 2001).

3. Charles Darwin, *On the Origin of Species by Means of Natural Selection, or the Preservation of Favoured Races in the Struggle for Life,* 1859. E-book, Electronic Text Center, Alderman Library, University of Virginia, p. 2.

4. Ibid.

5. Ibid., p. 84.

6. Ibid., p. 16.

7. Dennis O'Neil, "Darwin and Natural Selection," Palomar College, 2000, <http://daphne.palomar.edu/evolve/evolve_2.htm> (February 2, 2001).

8. D.R. Lees and E.R. Creed, "Industrial melanism in Biston betularia: the role of selective predation," *Journal of Animal Ecology,* vol. 44, 1975, pp. 67–83.

Chapter 2. Understanding Genes and Genetics

1. *Experiments in Plant Hybridization,* 1865, Mendel Web. Brown University, n.d., <http://www.netspace.org/MendelWeb/Mendel.html> (August 6, 2001).

2. Robert Shapiro, *The Human Blueprint* (New York: St. Martin's Press, 1991), p. 17.

3. Robert P. Wagner, "Understanding Inheritance," in *The Human Genome Project: Deciphering the Blueprint of Heredity,* ed. Necla Grant Cooper (Mill Valley, Calif.: University Science Books, 1994), p. 28.

4. Charles Darwin, *On the Origin of Species by Means of Natural Selection, or the Preservation of Favoured Races in the Struggle for Life,* 1859. E-book, Electronic Text Center, Alderman Library, University of Virginia, p. 128.

5. Wright, Robert, "James Watson and Francis Crick," *Time 100 Page,* n.d., <http://www.time.com/time/time100/scientist/profile/watsoncrick.html> (February 21, 2002).

Chapter 3. The Human Genome Project

1. *Understanding Our Genetic Inheritance: The U.S. Human Genome Project, The First Five Years: Fiscal Years 1991–1995,* April 1990, DOE/ER-0452P, NIH Publication No. 90-1590, <http://www.ornl.gov/hgmis/project/5yrplan/summary/html> (August 28, 2001).

2. Human Genome Program, U.S. Department of Energy, *To Know Ourselves,* 1996 <http://www.ornl.gov/hgmis/publicat/tko/02_why.html> (August 28, 2001).

3. White House press release, June 26, 2000.

4. "Five-Year Research Goals of the Human Genome Project," Oak Ridge National Laboratory, October 23, 1998, <http://www.ornl.gov/TechResources/Human_Genome/hg5yp/goal.html> (May 20, 2001).

5. Michio Kaku, *Visions: How Science Will Revolutionize the 21st Century* (New York: Doubleday, 1997), p.143.

6. Ibid.

Chapter 4. Health, Eugenics, and Genetic Counseling

1. *The Human Genome Project and the Future of Health Care,* ed. Thomas H. Murray, Mark A. Rothstein, and Robert F. Murray, Jr. (Indianapolis: Indiana University Press, 1996), p. vii.

2. William J. Polvino and W. French Anderson, "Medicine, Gene Therapy, and Society," in *The Human Genome Project and the Future of Health Care,* ed. Thomas H. Murray, Mark A. Rothstein, and Robert F. Murray, Jr. (Indianapolis: Indiana University Press, 1996), p. 47.

3. Ibid., p. 44.

4. Ibid., pp. 44–45.

5. Ibid., p. 53.

6. "The International Human Genome Project: Future Perspectives for Health for All," World Health Organization, n.d., <http://www.who.int/ncd/hgn/humgenp1.htm> (November 15, 2000).

7. Ibid.

8. Francis Galton, "Intellectual Capacity Transmitted by Descent," *MacMillan's Magazine,* November 1864–April 1865, pp. 318–327.

9. Michio Kaku, *Visions: How Science Will Revolutionize the 21st Century* (New York: Doubleday, 1997), p. 256.

10. Lenny Lapon, *Mass Murderers in White Coats: Psychiatric Genocide in Nazi Germany and the United States* (New York: Psychiatric Genocide Research Institute, 1986), < http://www.trufax.org/reports/lapon.html> (September 6, 2001).

11. Ibid.

12. Christopher Goodwin, "'Nobel sperm bank' babies . . . and how they grew: Case histories vary as children of wealthy man's 'genius' project come of age," *The Toronto Star,* January 16, 2000, <http://www.torstar.com/thestar/editorial/health/20000116BOD01b_BS-BRAINS.html> (February 15, 2001).

13. Kaku, p. 257.

14. Robert G. Resta, "Genetic Counseling: Coping with the Human Impact of Genetic Disease," Center for Perinatal Studies, n.d., <http://www.accessexcellence. com/AE/AEC/CC/counseling_background.html> (May 20, 2001).

15. Sheldon Reed, *Counseling in Medical Genetics,* (Philadelphia: W.B. Saunders Co., 1955), p. 14.

16. "American Society of Human Genetics Ad Hoc Committee on Genetic Counseling," *American Journal of Human Genetics* 27:240–242, 1975.

17. Thomas D. Bird, "Early-Onset Familial Alzheimer Disease," Gene Clinics, University of Washington, September 24, 1999, <http://www.geneclinics.org/ profiles/alzheimer-early/> (May 20, 2001).

Chapter 5. The Project's Effect on Industry and Science

1. Consulting Resources Corporation Newsletter, Spring 1999.

2. Peter G. Gesselin, "Clinton: Restrict Gene-Code Patents," Seattle Times Newssource, *Seattletimes.com,* February 11, 2000, <http://seattletimes.nwsource. com/news/nation-world/html98/clin_20000211.html> (October 30, 2001).

3. U.S. Supreme Court Opinion, *Diamond* v. *Chakrabarty,* 447 U.S. 303 (1980); *Diamond, commissioner of patents and trademarks* v. *Chakrabarty;* Certiorari to the United States Court of Customs and Patent Appeals. No. 79-136. Argued March 17, 1980, decided June 16, 1980.

4. "Genetically Engineered Food: Fast Facts," Environmental Media Services, n.d., <http://www.ems. org/biotech/sub2_food.html> (May 20, 2001).

5. "Genetically Engineered Food: Bt (or Insect-Resistant) Crops," Environmental Media Services, n.d., <http://www.ems.org/biotech/sub2_food_bt.html> (May 20, 2001).

6. "Pesticidal potatoes, terminator seeds and genetically mutated trees, oh my!" The Campaign to Label Genetically Engineered Foods, n.d., <http://www.thecampaign.org/brochuregrim.htm> (May 20, 2001).

7. "Tools for DNA Diagnostics," National Institute of Standards and Technology, Advanced Technology Program, August 1998, <http://www.atp.nist.gov/atp/97wp-dna.htm> (May 20, 2001).

8. Neil Caudle, "The Story of the Bones," University of North Carolina, 1998, <http://research.unc.edu/endeavors/spr98/bones.html> (May 18, 2001).

9. Brooke Eidenmiller, "Bioarcheologist Studies Skeletons for Clues to Past," UNC-CH News Service, No. 202, April 5, 2000.

10. Jeff Donn, "DNA Tests Show Earliest Humans Evolved in Africa," *Detroit Free Press,* December 7, 2000, <http://www.freep.com/news/nw/zdna7_20001207.htm> (May 20, 2001).

11. Josie Glausiusz, "Women on the Move," *Discover Magazine,* Science News Online, January 28, 1999, <http://www.discover.com/science_news/gthere.html?article=anthroscience.html> (May 20, 2001).

Chapter 6. Social Issues

1. Rita Delfiner, "Docs Crack Gene Code," *New York Post,* NYPOST.com, June 27, 2000, <http://208.248.87.252/06272000/6831.htm> (October 15, 2000).

2. "Government-Citizen Group Suggests Policies to Limit Genetic Discrimination in the Workplace," The National Human Genome Research Institute, n.d., <http://www.nhgri.nih.gov/NEWS/discrim.html> (May 20, 2001). (First appeared in *Science,* vol. 270: 391–393, 1995.)

3. Gary Heinlein, "Gene Study Raises Fears for Privacy: Protections Proposed To Ban Improper Use By Employers, Insurers," *The Detroit News,* February 15, 1999, p. D1.

4. Ibid.

5. Thomas Murray, "Ethical, Legal and Social Issues of the Human Genome Project: What to Do with What We Know," *Environmental Health Perspectives,* January 1994, vol. 102, no. 1, <http://ehpnet1.niehs.nih.gov/docs/1994/102-1/spheres.html> (August 28, 2001).

6. President Bill Clinton, Executive Order 13145, February 8, 2000.

7. David Korn, "Dangerous Intersections," *Issues in Science and Technology Online,* Fall 1996, <http://www.nap.edu/issues/13.1/korn.htm> (May 20, 2001).

8. Ibid.

9. The Genetic Privacy Act, Part A, Section 101-b, AKA "Guidelines for Protecting Privacy of Information Stored in Genetic Data Banks." Funded by the Ethical, Legal and Social Implications of the Human Genome Project, Office of Energy Research, U.S. Department of Energy, No. DE-FG02-93ER61626, 1995, <http://www.ornl.gov/hgmis/resource/privacy/privacy2.html/#A> (August 28, 2001).

10. Korn.

11. Ibid.

12. Ibid.

13. Naomi Aoki, "BU Cancels Deal To Sell Patient Data," *The Boston Globe,* December 29, 2000, p. C1.

14. Mae-Wan Ho, "Human Genome—The Biggest Sellout in Human History," Institute of Science in Society, <http://I-sis.org/humangenome.shtml> (August 28, 2001).

15. Ibid.

16. "Position Paper on Human Germline Manipulation," The Council for Responsible Genetics Human Genetics Council, Fall 1992, <http://www.gene-watch.org/programs/Position_Germline.html> (May 20, 2001).

17. Ibid.

18. Ibid.

19. Darryl Macer, "What the genome project means for society," *Ethical Challenges as We Approach the End of the Human Genome Project,* ed. Darryl R.J. Macer, Institute of Biological Sciences, University of Tsukuba, 2000, pp. 107–121, <http://www.biol.tsukuba.ac.jp/~macer/chgp/chgp107.html> (May 20, 2001).

20. Ibid.

Chapter 7. Legal and Ethical Issues

1. *Diamond* v. *Chakrabarty,* 447 U.S. 303; 100 S. Ct. 2204; 1980 U.S. LEXIS 112; 65 L. Ed. 2d 144; 206 U.S.P.Q. (BNA) 193 (1980).

2. United States. Congressional Senate. S.300 1999, A Bill, Genetic Information Nondiscrimination in Health Insurance Act of 1999. [Introduced in the U.S. Senate; March 26, 2000.] Washington, D.C.: U.S. Government Printing Office. DOCID: sbo774f.rtf.

3. *Tommie Lee Andrews* v. *State of Florida,* No. 87-2166, October 20, 1988.

4. Eric Lander, "DNA Fingerprinting: Science, Law, and the Ultimate Identifier," in *The Code of Codes: Scientific and Social Issues in the Human Genome Project,* ed. Daniel J. Kevles and Leroy Hood (Cambridge, Mass.: Harvard University Press, 1992), pp. 191–210.

5. Janet Reno, "Message from the Attorney General," in Edward Connors, Thomas Lundregan, Neal Miller, and Tom McEwen, *Convicted by Juries, Exonerated by Science: Case Studies in the Use of DNA Evidence to Establish Innocence After Trial,* U.S. Department of Justice, Office of Justice Programs and the National Institute of Justice, June 1996, p. iii.

6. Janet Reno, keynote address to The American Academy of Forensic Sciences, Nashville, Tenn., February 21, 1996.

7. U.S. Constitution. XIII Ammendment.

8. "Civil Rights Act of 1965," Title VII, SEC. 2000e-2 [Section 703], a-1.

9. "New EEOC Guidelines Clarify Disability," *Human Genome News* 7(2): 4, July–August 1995, <http://www. ornl.gov/hgmis/publicat/hgn/v7n2/4eeocada.html> (May 20, 2001).

10. The National Human Genome Research Institute, "Ethical, Legal and Social Implications (ELSI): Program Areas," National Human Genome Research Institute, n.d., <http://www.nhgri.nih.gov/About_NHGRI/Der/Elsi/high_priority.html> (May 20, 2001).

11. Ibid.

12. Michio Kaku, *Visions: How Science Will Revolutionize the 21st Century* (New York: Anchor Books, 1997), p. 220.

13. Catherine Baker, "Your Genes, Your Choices: Exploring the Issues Raised by Genetic Research," Science + Literacy for Health, AAAS Directorate for Education and Human Resources, n.d., <http://www.ornl.gov/hgmis/publicat/genechoice/7_dr.html> (May 20, 2001).

Chapter 8. A Look to the Future

1. "Scientists to Clone Humans." About.com, 2001, <http://lds.about.com/religion/lds/library/weekly/aa013001a.htm> (May 20, 2001).

2. Rick Weiss, "Mass Firm's Disclosure Renews Cloning Debate," *The Washington Post,* November 27, 2001, p. A03.

Glossary

adenine (adeninethymine)—One of the four basic nitrogenous bases that make up DNA. Adenine always bonds with thymine.

allele—One of two genes that can be located at the same place on a chromosome and result in different traits.

base pair—Two nitrogenous bases that are bound together. Adenine binds with thymine and guanine binds with cytosine. Strands of DNA are held together by these weak bonds between bases.

base sequence—The order of bases in a molecule of DNA.

chromosome—A narrow, threadlike object found in the nucleus of plant and animal cells. Chromosomes are made up of DNA and proteins. They carry the genes and have the ability to replicate themselves.

clone—An exact copy made of some living organism.

cytosine—One of the four basic nitrogenous bases that make up DNA. Cytosine always bonds with guanine.

DNA (deoxyribonucleic acid)—A chemical that carries the genetic information in the cell. It is arranged in the shape of a double helix.

DNA sequence—The order of base pairs in a section of DNA.

double helix—The shape of two bonded strands of DNA.

epigenesist—One who believes that life forms from an undifferentiated, simple mass by differentiating into more complex organs or parts.

eugenics—A movement to improve the human race through selective breeding.

gene—A hereditary unit. A gene is located on a chromosome and determines a particular characteristic.

gene mapping—Determining the location of genes on a molecule of DNA.

genetic code—A sequence of nucleotides.

genetics—The study of how genes transmit characteristics from parents to offspring.

genome—The total genetic information in the chromosomes of any living thing.

genomic sequence—The order of all the nitrogenous bases along a section of DNA.

guanine—One of the four basic nitrogenous bases that make up DNA. Guanine always bonds with cytosine.

homunculus—A very tiny, fully formed human being, which according to some preformationists was present in the male of a species and grew to full size in the female, and according to others was present in the female and was fertilized by the male.

Human Genome Project—A collective effort among various organizations, governments, scientists, and companies to map the entire human DNA sequence.

hybrid—Offspring produced by breeding dissimilar parents. If, for example, you breed a bush that only produces red roses with a bush that only produces white roses, the resulting rose bush would be a hybrid.

mutation—A change in the structure of DNA for an organism that can be passed on to future generations.

nitrogenous base—A base that contains nitrogen.

nucleic acid—A large molecule of nucleotides.

nucleotide—The combination of a base pair, a phosphate molecule, and a sugar molecule.

nucleus—A structure inside a cell that contains all genetic material for an organism.

preformationists—People who believed that babies were preformed before conception. (See "homunculus.")

protein—Any of a number of large molecules common to all living things; product of a gene.

RNA (ribonucleic acid)—A chemical with a similar structure to DNA, which is found inside cells.

sequencing—Determining the order of base pairs in DNA or RNA, or determining the order of amino acids in proteins.

single-gene disorder—A disease or malady caused by only one allele or gene.

terminator technology—Techniques used to genetically engineer organisms (particularly crops, such as corn) to be sterile so that they can not reproduce.

thymine—One of the four basic nitrogenous bases that make up DNA. Thymine always bonds with adenine.

trait—A characteristic, such as hair color, height, intelligence, and so on.

Further Reading

Aaseng, Nathan. *Genetics: Unlocking the Secrets of Life.* Minneapolis: Oliver Press, 1996.

Bodmer, Walter, and Robin McKie. *The Book of Man: The Human Genome Project and the Quest to Discover our Genetic Heritage.* New York: Oxford University Press, 1997.

Brown, Austen. *Genomes.* New York: John Wiley & Sons, 1999.

Cooper, Necla Grant, editor. *The Human Genome Project: Deciphering the Blueprint of Heredity.* Mill Valley, Calif.: University Science Books, 1994.

Davies, Kevin. *Cracking the Genome: Inside the Race to Unlock Human DNA.* New York: Free Press, 2001.

Edelson, Edward. *Francis Crick & James Watson: And the Building Blocks of Life.* New York: Oxford University Press, 1998.

Kevles, Daniel J., and Leroy Hood, editors. *The Code of Codes: Scientific and Social Issues in the Human Genome Project.* Cambridge: Harvard University Press, 1992.

Klare, Roger. *Gregor Mendel: Father of Genetics.* Springfield, N.J.: Enslow Publishers, Inc., 1997.

Marshall, Elizabeth L. *Human Genome Project: Cracking the Code Within Us.* New York: Franklin Watts, 1996.

Peters, Ted, editor. *Genetics: Issues of Social Justice.* New York: Pilgrim Press, 1998.

Internet Addresses

Human Genome Project Information
<http://www.ornl.gov/hgmis>

National Institutes of Health, National Human Genome Research Institute
<http://www.genome.gov>

World Health Organization, Human Genetics Web site
<http://www.who.int/ncd/hgn>

Index